Kirstin von Glasow

111 Coffee Shops in London That You Must Not Miss

D1079297

emons:

© Emons Verlag GmbH
All rights reserved
© all photos: Kirstin von Glasow
Design: Eva Kraskes, based on a design
by Lübbeke | Naumann | Thoben
Edited by Katrina Fried
Maps: altancicek.design, www.altancicek.de
Layout Cover: Nina Schäfer
Cover icons: iStockphoto.com/anna42fa, iStockphoto.com/missbobbit,
iStockphoto.com/redcollegiya, iStockphoto.com/iStockFinland
Printing and binding: B.O.S.S Medien GmbH, Goch
Printed in Germany 2015
ISBN 978-3-95451-614-8
First edition

Did you enjoy it? Do you want more?
Join us in uncovering new places around the world on:
www.111places.com

Foreword

For many years, London didn't have a coffee culture worth mentioning. After all, the English were known as a nation of tea drinkers. There were very few opportunities to enjoy a refined cappuccino amid beautiful surroundings as has long been customary in Vienna, Paris, and other continental cities.

When coffee chains arrived in Europe, they quickly filled this gap and became a ubiquitous feature on the English High Street. Less obtrusive but equally important is the "third wave" coffee revolution that's taken place in the capital over the past two decades. Triggered by antipodean immigrants who were used to getting a good flat white in every corner cafe (Australia is reputed to have some of the best coffee in the world), more and more independent coffee shops have opened here in recent years.

London not only emulated Australian coffee culture but also developed its own indigenous scene, with cafes in such creative locales as public toilets and bike shops. Small local roasters, often in combination with cafes, produce an amazing variety of high-quality roasts. Who would have thought 20 years ago that London would become one of the most exciting places in the world to drink coffee?

Coffee lovers here are now spoiled with an array of excellent options, often finding equally brilliant cosmopolitan food to accompany their espresso. As there are so many wonderful cafes to choose from, the selection in this book is necessarily a personal one and every reader is encouraged to discover his or her own favourite.

It is often forgotten that the first London coffee house was opened in 1652 by Pasqua Rose, inspiring a boom in coffee culture that lasted for 200 years. The London cafe of today can be seen as a reincarnation of the 17th-century original, which was described as a place of "sparkling conviviality, and stimulating, wide-ranging conversation powered by caffeine and innovative wit."

111 Coffee Shops

126

1__ 46b Espresso Hut

Keeping it personal

Filled with plants and cuttings in different-sized containers and old tins, 46b Espresso Hut is a friendly and welcoming oasis on a rainy morning. The beautiful, large shop window was the first thing Eva Kostelidou and Dominic Rich fell in love with when they found this space. For years Eva had planned to open her own cafe, and talked her partner Dom into doing it with her. They looked for a long time before finally settling here on Brooksby's Walk in 2012.

The walls are painted white, and recycled crates and a long bench running along one wall serve as seating in the small, narrow space. Eva had already worked in coffee shops for several years and knew she wanted to make Square Mile their house espresso. She likes that it's seasonal and that they often change the blend. The milk is from Northiam Dairy, bread and brownies are by E5 Bakehouse, and pastries come from Yeast Bakery.

Eva and Dom's aim is to have as much homemade or locally sourced as possible. To that end, they offer seasonal jams from London Borough of Jam made by their friend Lillie in her kitchen just up the road; Clapton Honey, which is produced in someone's garden a few streets away; and Rubies in the Rubble, chutneys made with left-over fruits and vegetables from Borough Market. The salad greens are grown on nearby Hackney Marsh. Breakfast dishes, sandwiches, cakes, and soups are all prepared in the tiny kitchen behind the counter. Some of the specials, such as Dimitri's Spanakopita, come from Eva's homeland of Greece.

The customers here are mostly locals. Homerton Hospital is just around the corner and patients and staff appreciate having a nice cafe in the neighbourhood. Some have asked for cuttings from Eva's Beefsteak plants, and in return bring her cuttings from their own gardens. "Making everything ourselves is just more personal. It's part of us, and people appreciate that."

Address 46b Brooksby's Walk, E 9 6DA, Tel +44(0)7702063172, dmnc_rch@yahoo.co.uk, www.46b-espressohut.co.uk | **Getting there** London Overground, Stop Homerton | **Hours** Mon–Fri 7.30am–6pm, Sat 9am–6pm, Sun 10am–5pm | **Tip** On Sundays, the nearby Chatsworth Road Market is worth exploring.

2 Algerian Coffee Stores

Coffee around the world

Follow the smell of freshly roasted coffee down Old Compton Street in the heart of Soho and it will lead you straight to the Algerian Coffee Stores. You can't miss the vivid red façade and the front window displaying old-fashioned coffee and tea paraphernalia. Enter the shop and you'll find yourself seduced not only by the aroma but also the charming interior, which is full of original features, such as an old scale, faded photographs, and wooden shelves crowded with glass jars containing various coffees and teas.

The store was founded in 1887 by Mr Hassan, who is believed to have been one of the first Algerians to come to London. In 1926, he sold it to a Belgian gentleman who, in 1948, sold it to Marisa Crocetta's grandfather. Today, Marisa, her sister, and her father all work here. Marisa's father taught her everything about the trade while on the job. The Crocettas offer about 80 different kinds of coffee and 100 types of tea as well as confectionaries from Italy, France, South America, Turkey, and beyond; spices; and home brewing accessories, from coffee grinders and milk frothers to filter papers and tea infusers. With beans roasted to their specifications just outside London, they create house blends that you won't find anywhere else.

You will experience the agony of options here: Should you choose a blend or a single origin? Organic, spiced, decaf, or raw? Australian, African, Indian, Indonesian, or South American? Also worth trying are the rare and unusual coffees they stock, such as one from Vietnam, chocolatey and strong, or the sought-after Jamaica Blue Mountain, of which only small quantities are produced each year. And while you're at it, pick up some tea as well – this is London, after all. Chinese, Indian, Japanese, green teas, white teas, flowers and petals … prepare to start your journey around the world – one cup at a time.

Address 52 Old Compton Street, W1D 4PB, Tel +44(0)2074372480, algcoffee.co.uk |
Getting there Northern and Piccadilly Line, Stop Leicester Square | Hours Mon–Wed
9am–7pm, Thur–Fri 9am–9pm, Sat 9am–8pm | Tip Another classic Soho institution is
Lina Stores (18 Brewer Street), an Italian delicatessen dating back to the 1940s.

3 _ Anima e Cuore

"Soul and heart"

It's easy to overlook Anima e Cuore ("soul and heart" in Italian) on Kentish Town Road. The exterior is unassuming and the narrow inside space is dominated by large refrigerated counters, the first of which is filled with a variety of homemade frozen delights, from mango ice cream to the darkest chocolate sorbet. You might therefore assume that Anima e Cuore is simply a gelateria, but continue toward the back of the cafe and you quickly realise there is much more to come. Ice cream is followed by colourful macaroons, choux pastry, brioche, two different kinds of tiramisu, and a scrumptious ricotta and mascarpone cake, not to mention a dazzling array of 20 different biscuits. They even make their own croissants and pain au chocolat. Past the sweets you arrive at the savouries, which include arancini, lasagne, and giant cheeses. Behind the counter you can glimpse the pasta machine, where ravioli are filled with pumpkin and amaretti or spinach and ricotta right in front of your eyes.

"All this is made here in the small kitchen," explains Mustapha Mouflih, who owns the shop together with Alessandro Altoni. Both chefs have worked in a variety of top restaurants in London. When they finally realised their dream of opening their own place in summer 2014, they brought a wealth of experience and a passion for Italian food to the venture. Mustapha's family hails from Morocco but he was born in southern Italy and lived for many years near Lake Garda. He sources a number of their products from Italy, be it the Parmigiano–Reggiano, which can only be so called if it is produced in the region; or the coffee from Caffé Diemme in Padova.

Mustapha and Alessandro aimed to bring a taste of Italy to London – and have succeeded beautifully. Word has already spread in the neighbourhood that if it's good coffee and heart-and-soul-warming Italian food you want, Anima e Cuore is the right place for you.

Address 129 Kentish Town Road, NW1 8PB, Tel +44(0)2072672410, www.facebook.com/pages/Anima-e-cuore-nw1/728859107177663 | **Getting there** Northern Line, Stop Camden Town or Kentish Town | **Hours** Mon–Thur 8am–7pm, Fri–Sat 10am–11pm, Sun 11am–8pm | **Tip** If you are in need of a lock, tool, or window fittings, pay a visit to the nearby shop Franchi (144–145 Kentish Town Road), the local specialist for ironmongery.

4_ Arlo & Moe

Give it a shake

The 1950s American ice-cream parlour look – complete with pastel colours and a collection of cute animal salt and pepper shakers on the tables – gives this local cafe a special flair. Julie O'Neill and Jamie Mockridge opened Arlo & Moe in September 2012. In Julie's words: "It has been amazing since day one, just busy, busy, busy!"

Before Arlo & Moe's, Julie had a cupcake company. Jamie is Julie's brother-in-law and in addition to his many other careers, he was once a baker. As family members sometimes do, they started talking. Julie had always wanted to open a coffee shop and it turned out that Jamie shared the same dream, so they quit their jobs and gave it a shot.

With their backgrounds, the cakes are naturally brilliant, all made in-house except for some pastries supplied by a French bakery, and the panettone, which comes directly from Verona. Be sure to try the Chocolate Guinness Cake or the Raspberry Bakewell Cake (or both!). Julie also has an online custom cake business called Julie Madly Deeply, where you can order amazing desserts in all shapes and colours for every occasion.

Arlo & Moe serves a full breakfast with many options, including scrambled eggs, porridge, and French toast. The signature dishes here are the Sexy Toasts, with different savoury and sweet toppings (a popular choice is avocado and feta). Two different soups, as well as quiches and frittatas, are usually on offer for lunch. Everything is cooked on the premises and the ingredients are sourced locally.

As for the coffee, it comes from a small roaster on Brockley Market called Dark Fluid, which supplies a couple of stalls and cafes in the area. The customers are a real mix, mostly locals: workers from the surrounding offices during the week and groups of friends, couples, and families on the weekend. Children love it here. What kid wouldn't want to use a cute cat or dog shaker to salt their eggs?

Address 340 Brockley Road, SE 4 2BT, Tel +448(0)7749667207 or +44(0)7799142263, www.facebook.com/pages/Arlo-Moe/447851225239416 | Getting there Thameslink or London Overground, Stop Crofton Park or Brockley | Hours Mon–Fri 8am–4.30pm, Sat 9am–4pm, Sun 10am–4pm | Tip Rivoli Ballroom (350 Brockley Road) has a stunning 1950s space where you can attend costume balls, jive and swing parties, and other dance events.

5 The Attendant

Designed with efficiency

It's easy to mistake this coffee shop for something else. After all, 27A Foley Street was built in the Victorian era as a men's toilet. As you descend into the cast-iron cage, you find yourself inside a narrow men's lavatory, still complete with urinals, cistern, and hand dryer. But this former privy now houses a bustling cafe with room for up to 33 people.

Owner Ryan De Oliveira never imagined running a coffee shop in a restroom. Before opening the Attendant he'd worked in finance and had a friend who managed a nightclub. Both were at crossroads in their lives and needed a change. Over lunch, they decided to go into the coffee business together – but there were a couple of obstacles to overcome. For one thing, they had no experience, and for another, it took them ages to find a location. They were finally offered the Attendant, which was already a cafe at the time. Built around 1890 and closed in the 1960s, it had been derelict for 50 years and was a complete mess. The cage above was covered with 11 layers of paint that had to be stripped before it could be refinished. The previous owner had already invested in a kitchen in the old attendant's office. Unfortunately there were only 14 seats in the cafe and after just three months, Ryan realized they needed more room. So they removed the kitchen, installed more seating, and maximized every inch of space.

These days, all the food is prepared off-site and delivered each morning. The coffee is by Caravan and the Attendant is especially proud of the creamy milk with natural fat content that it uses, which comes from Ivy House Farm in Somerset and perfectly augments the taste of the coffee. There's a lot of attention to detail here, including whiteboards on the walls that customers can use during their meetings. After all, a men's toilet needs to be designed and run with efficiency!

Address Downstairs, 27a Foley Street, W1W 6DY, Tel +44(0)2076373794,
info@the-attendant.com, www.the-attendant.com | Getting there Northern Line,
Stop Goodge Street | Hours Mon–Fri 8am–6pm, Sat 10am–5pm | Tip Stop in at
Scandinavian Kitchen (61 Titchfield Street), a Swedish grocer, where you can fill your
larder with Nordic produce.

6__Bea's of Bloomsbury

Home of the original duffin

Indulgence is the word that comes to mind when you peek through the shop window of Bea's of Bloomsbury. There are always mountains of jewel-coloured cupcakes: heart-shaped cakes for Valentine's Day, meringue bunnies and chicks at Easter, and marshmallow mushrooms on chocolate soil in the fall.

Treat yourself to afternoon tea – it needs to be booked in advance – in the small pale blue space that is inventively lit by hanging teapots. You have three options, all of them containing various assortments of sandwiches, scones, cupcakes, marshmallows, brownies, and blondies. Or, if that's more than you bargained for, simply enjoy a coffee by Square Mile or a gunpowder tea accompanied by one of their amazing pastries.

Bea's was conceived and created by Bea Vo, an American from New York. Before opening the cafe in 2008, she worked as the head pastry chef for Nobu restaurant. Apart from Bloomsbury, she owns two other cafes, in Farringdon and St Paul's. The Bloomsbury venue houses the main kitchen. All the cakes are made here and delivered every morning to the two other shops. You can also order special occasion or wedding cakes on her website.

Bea is a very creative baker, having invented several new types of baked goods such as the "townie," a cross between a tart and a brownie, and the "duffin," a hybrid of a doughnut and a muffin. It's made from buttermilk and nutmeg batter, filled with jam, dipped in butter, and rolled in sugar. It's a customer favourite, and Bea features it in her cookbook *Tea with Bea*. When Starbucks introduced a similar product and their supplier tried to trademark the name *duffin* in 2013, Bea's loyal duffin fans voiced their outrage on Twitter and other social media. She was able to prove she used the name for her doughnut–muffin first.

So tuck in, because life is short and you never know how long you'll be able to call your duffin a duffin!

Address 44 Theobalds Road, WC1X 8NW, Tel +44(0)2072428330, cakes@beasofbloomsbury.com, www.beasofbloomsbury.com | **Getting there** Central Line or Piccadilly Line, Stop Holborn or Chancery Lane | **Hours** Mon–Sun 9am–5pm | **Tip** If the weather is nice, enjoy a take-away sandwich or pastry in nearby Gray's Inn Gardens (open to the public Mon–Fri 12–2.30pm).

7__Bear + Wolf

Once upon a coffee shop …

A young family that's just moved to Tufnell Park can hardly miss this cafe, which opened in June 2014. Its logo, which consists of a kind bear and a mean wolf, was designed by a branding expert who's a friend of the owner, Matthew Neel. Matthew wanted a name from a fairy tale for the cafe without it being pink and cute, so he settled on two of the nastiest animals in the world of classic children's stories. They made badges with the logo, which were sold out immediately.

Matthew used a similar no-nonsense approach when he created the cafe's spacious interior, with its industrial lighting and large community tables. The family-friendly atmosphere here is wonderful, but the ultimate draw for parents with toddlers is the room in the back. It is filled with games, books, and toys to keep the little ones busy, giving not only parents a break but allowing other customers to relax undisturbed or even to work here. There is also plenty of "parking space" available for buggies.

If you're an exhausted mum or dad in need of a caffeine fix, Bear + Wolf brews excellent coffee. Matthew prefers a darker roast and uses Ozone beans. Bear + Wolf's menu (they also have a separate kids' menu) focuses on simple breakfast and lunch dishes, including sandwiches, granola, buttermilk waffles, a soup of the day, tarts, and shepherd's pie. The cakes are made by Matthew's sister-in-law and the amazing juices and smoothies – try the All–Day Breakfast Smoothie with banana, dates, oats and yoghurt – are not only very healthy, "some of them are especially good for pregnant women," assures Matthew.

There is a simple explanation as to why Bear + Wolf is so accommodating to all ages. Matthew's daughter was four years old when he founded the cafe and he wanted to create a social and relaxed place where parents could meet one another outside the nursery.

Address 153 Fortess Road, NW5 2HR, Tel +44(0)2036011900, bearandwolfcafe.com | Getting there Northern Line, Stop Tufnell Park | Hours Mon–Fri 7.30am–5.30pm, Sat–Sun 8.30am–5.30pm | Tip Those expecting a child might enjoy a visit to the Active Birth Centre (25 Bickerton Road). There you can do pregnancy yoga and get advice on natural childbirth.

8   Bel & Nev
Small and local

Parallel to busy Chamberlayne Road, a small terrace with independent retailers leads to Kensal Rise Station. Bella Baistow-Clare Datora and her husband Nevio Datora Filho opened their little coffee shop here in September 2014. At night, the exterior of the cafe resembles an Edward Hopper painting. A glimpse inside reveals a red-and-white 1950s kitchen cabinet that used to stand in Bella and Nevio's home.

Both are trained chefs and wanted to serve what they liked to cook: simple, fresh, seasonal food of good quality. Running a pop–up cafe at Hay Festival for eight years helped them prepare for opening their own place. There weren't many good coffee shops in the area and Bella believes that "Kensal Rise is only just coming into good coffee." They use beans from Union Hand-Roasted, which inspires a lot of compliments from customers.

Given their proximity to the station, they get a lot of commuters stopping in for a quick caffeine fix on the way to work. But their delicious breakfasts are worth slowing down for: from simple toast with homemade jam or porridge to spicy slow-cooked beans with red peppers, chorizo, and feta cheese. Smashed avocado on toast comes with chilli jam made by Bella's mum. They also sell a range of house pickles and jams and serve them with sandwiches and toasts. Nevio bakes all the cakes. Regulars particularly love his caramel brownies and the toasted banana bread with butter.

The couple likes keeping it small and local, partly because they want to make time for their 3-year-old daughter. But they do plan to get an alcohol license and start serving simple food and beer in the evenings. Bella feels at home on this stretch of the terrace with its variety of independent shops – the barber has been here for 30 years. "It's a friendly community and people have been really nice to us. A lot of them say that they feel like they're sitting in our kitchen here."

Address 15 Station Terrace, NW10 5RX Tel +44(0)2037208825,
www.facebook.com/bellaandnevio | **Getting there** London Overground, Stop Kensal Rise |
Hours Mon–Sat 8am–5pm, Sun 10am–4pm | **Tip** Nearby Kensal Green Cemetery is one
of London's Victorian cemeteries and displays many gothic monuments. Freddie Mercury
and Ingrid Bergman were cremated here.

9 __ Betty's Coffee
The living room of Dalston

"It was an accident," says Betty Sharp, when asked how she came to own a cafe. "I lived in the area for fifteen years and I thought we should have a coffee shop here, so I opened one." This small establishment on Kingsland Road in Dalston is defined by its relaxed atmosphere. Wood floors, exposed brickwork, and vivid blue walls open to a small back room dominated by a colorful mural with palm trees. Evocative of a comfortable living room, it's a lovely place to sit and linger, and often strangers strike up conversations while enjoying their coffee or sandwiches.

Betty's opens at 8:30am and offers freshly prepared and hearty breakfasts like bacon, egg, and rocket on toast, or a fried egg and wilted spinach on a cheddar-and-chive bagel. She also has a small lunch menu of made-to-order quesadillas and halloumi burgers. The cafe serves Redchurch, the signature espresso blend from Allpress, a roaster that was originally established in New Zealand and opened an outpost in London in 2010.

An additional plus is that Betty's has had an alcohol license since 2014. From Wednesday to Saturday the space turns into an intimate bar in the evenings. The absence of loud music makes it especially enjoyable for those seeking a place to talk and unwind. In addition to specialty cocktails and spirits, Betty's serves two kinds of London beer – one ale and one lager – which rotate every few months.

Even when it was just a coffee shop, Betty's hosted the occasional music event. Since becoming a bar by night, such happenings are a regular feature. On Wednesdays, customers can bring their favourite records, and on Thursdays, the stage is open to anyone who wants to share a piece of performance art. All of the live music is recorded and can be listened to on the coffee shop's website. Once a month, on a Friday evening, the art displayed on the walls changes. All in all, a pretty busy living room!

Address 510b Kingsland Road, E 8 4AE, Tel +44(0)7939228592, bettyscoffee@gmail.com, www.bettyscoffee.co.uk | Getting there London Overground, Stop Dalston Kingsland | Hours Mon – Tue 8.30am – 4pm, Wed 8.30am – 6pm, Thur 8.30am – 11pm, Fri 8.30am – midnight, Sat 10am – midnight, Sun 10am – 11pm | Tip On a nice summer's day, De Beauvoir Square, with its beautiful formal rose garden, offers a welcome break from busy Kingsland Road.

10 __ Birdhouse

Australia and Cuba unite

South-West London isn't exactly known as a hub for specialty coffee – but there is a light on the horizon. Three years ago, former graphic designers Cameron Rosenbrock and Alexei Morales opened Birdhouse on St John's Hill. Cameron is from Melbourne and Alexei is Cuban. The cafe is a delightful blend of their different heritages.

The shop was previously a medical practice, so they had to start from scratch. The partners designed and built everything themselves, repurposing objects along the way, like turning old lockers into shelves. The walls are grey, brought to life with splashes of yellow cups and signs. Birds decorate vintage plates, and there are old-school avian charts and other bird–themed decorations throughout the space. Cameron chose the name Birdhouse in memory of his dad's favourite song: "Birdhouse in your Soul," by They Might Be Giants.

The food is also an amalgam of their two cultures. There are Australian items such as mashed avocado with feta and mint on toast, corn fritters, smoked salmon, several egg dishes, and on the sweet side – Lamington cake: a traditional Australian cake coated with chocolate and coconut. Typical Cuban dishes offered are *bocaditos* – Cuban sandwiches – with different fillings including Serrano ham, oven-roasted tomatoes, and Iberico cheese.

Since Cameron comes from Melbourne – where it's actually a struggle to find a bad cup of coffee – the choice of beans was essential. For their house espresso, they selected the Climpson Estate Espresso Blend with 50 percent Ethiopian Sidamo Sasaba and 50 percent Brazilian Daterra. They also offer different single origins for filter coffee, using AeroPress. The tea is by Waterloo Tea, with varieties like Yunnan Breakfast, Tangerine Ginger, and Cinnamon Spice.

Neighbours and locals appreciate the Aussie-Cuban fusion and love the all-day breakfasts, especially on weekends.

Birdhouse.

Coffee
bocaditos
& cakes.

Address 23 St John's Hill, SW11 1SZ, Tel +44(0)2072286663, info@birdhou.se,
www.birdhou.se | **Getting there** London Overground, Stop Clapham Junction | **Hours**
Mon−Fri 7am−4pm, Sat−Sun 9am−5pm | **Tip** Battersea Arts Centre (Lavender Hill)
houses theatre and dance events in a beautiful historic building.

11 The Black Lab Coffee House

A true brotherhood

The Black Lab can be found on the south side of Clapham Common behind a busy bus stop. The beautiful wooden coffeemaker in the window hints at the brilliant brew you'll get here.

Inside the cafe, your eye will be immediately drawn to the display of tasty sandwiches and cakes on the counter. But first, order your espresso, cappuccino, or latte: the house blend is Opus, from Alchemy, with notes of chocolate, hazelnut, and red currant. They also have guest blends from other roasters, such as Campbell & Syme, and offer cold-brew filter coffees. If you're lactose intolerant, try the organic almond milk.

Although coffee-focused, this cafe doesn't simply cater to those hunting for a perfect flat white: they also make a mean chai latte and a lovely hot chocolate. In the summer they offer delicious "cold-pressed" juices, with flavour combinations such as cucumber, kale, apple, mint, and lime.

The gourmet toasted sandwiches on potato-and-rosemary sourdough are all excellent. The New Vegan is made with falafel, humus, and avocado, and the Chicken Club with pulled chicken, crispy bacon, and avocado. Feeling peckish for something sweet? Try the exotic Hummingbird Cake with mangos, passion fruit, pineapples, and a scrumptious cheesecake icing, or the creamy triple-layered red velvet cake, which is rumoured to be the best in town.

So who's behind all these offerings? The Black Lab was founded in July 2010 by three brothers: Matt, James, and Alex Goodman. Matt worked in Italy for a year and then in cafes, restaurants, and bars in Canada. When he returned to London, he wanted to do something coffee related, and the Black Lab evolved from there. Matt is the head barista and James does pretty much everything else. Together they manage to serve some of the best coffee in Clapham.

Address 18 Clapham Common Southside, SW4 7AB, Tel +44(0)2077388441, james@blacklabcoffee.com, www.blacklabcoffee.com | **Getting there** Northern Line, Stop Clapham Common | **Hours** Mon–Tue 7.15am–5.30pm, Wed 7.15am–4.30pm, Thur–Fri 7.15am–5.30pm, Sat 8.30am–5pm, Sun 9am–5pm | **Tip** Nearby Clapham Picturehouse (76 Venn Street) is a popular art–house cinema with a bar.

12 Bread and Bean

A gem in Archway

The area around Archway tube station is not exactly known for its wealth of cosy coffee shops. With seven bus routes that commence or end here, most people are in a rush and grab their coffee on the run. Bona Sadiku and Jose Granja lived in the neighbourhood with their small daughter for several years, and they were well aware of the lack of places to linger and enjoy a good brew. Both were keen for a career change and loved coffee. They looked for a location where they could open a friendly local cafe. "Actually," admits Bona, "we wanted a place where we would like to go."

In December 2012, they opened Bread and Bean on Junction Road in a former greasy spoon. With only a small budget and the help of their friends, they've created a light, welcoming space with copper lamps and a wooden counter. The main focus is on the coffee: a blend for lovers of strong coffee from Union Roasters. They also offer a hearty breakfast and lunch menu with porridge, full English breakfast, eggs Benedict, and a kid's option of boiled egg and soldiers. For lunch try the fish-finger sandwich, roasted pork belly, or soups and salads that are made daily in the kitchen downstairs and changed seasonally. Many of the cakes are also baked in-house, such as the Orange Victoria Sponge Cake. The bread and pastries come from Sally Clarke's Bakery or the Bread Factory.

The cafe quickly found many loyal customers among the locals and was named "Archway's first decent coffee shop." It became so successful that Bona and Jose were able to open another location in a former pub in Holloway. The Spoke is a cycle-friendly cafe serving burgers and the tried-and-trusted Union Roast.

Bona realized that establishing an independent cafe really could make a difference to a neighbourhood. A real estate agent told her that even the house prices have gone up since she and Jose opened Bread and Bean.

Address 37 Junction Road, N19 5QU, Tel +44(0)2072630667, www.twitter.com/ breadandbean37 | **Getting there** Northern Line, Stop Archway | **Hours** Mon–Fri 7.30am–6pm, Sat–Sun 8.30am–6pm | **Tip** On nearby Highgate Hill, a small statue of a cat in a cage commemorates Richard Whittington, a famous medieval Lord Mayor of London. According to legend, he started his career at this very spot, aided by his clever cat.

13__Brill

Little New York

Jeremy Brill gets up very early every morning, cycles to Brick Lane Bagel Bake, picks up 80 to 100 bagels, and brings them to Brill. Why? It all started back in 1999, when Jeremy first opened Brill as a CD and record store. It was very successful for about five years but then sales dropped off and Jeremy decided to evolve the business. He was excited by antipodean-style coffee and cafes. He also liked traditional Jewish delis. Somehow these three passions combined into one venture: "Music, coffee, and bagels!"

Three years ago he refurbished the interior of the cafe to create more space for food prep. It became less record shop and more coffee shop. Music still has an integral part to play at Brill, however; there's a nice selection of classical, jazz, and English folk CDs for sale as well as some vinyl.

But back to the bagels: Jeremy did a lot of research before he opened the cafe and discovered the best bagels in London were to be found at Brick Lane Bagel Bake. Unfortunately, they don't deliver, so Jeremy fetches the bagels himself. With them, Brill offers a classic salmon and cream cheese, as well as an antipodean bagel/toast with avocado, feta, and dukkah, and the "Everything Bagel" with lots of vegetables. The cakes are baked by Arianna from Bittersweet Bakers.

Jeremy's motto is to keep it simple, do it well, and use the best ingredients. Brill has sold coffee roasted by Union since the beginning, and Jeremy's barista skills have become much more scientific over the years – he weighs each shot to guarantee a consistent quality. Brill's customers are mainly locals who appreciate this attention to detail and show up as many as four times a day for their caffeine fix. "They also influence us, for instance, by asking for something like a salad on the menu. We have an incredibly loyal clientele here and it really feels like a New York neighbourhood!"

Address 27 Exmouth Market, EC1R 4QL, Tel +44(0)78339757, www.exmouth.london/brill | Getting there Northern Line, Stop Angel | Hours Mon–Fri 7.30am–6pm, Sat 9am–6pm | Tip Just down the road you'll find Caravan (11–13 Exmouth Market), the Kiwi–run artisan coffee-roaster-*cum*-restaurant.

14 Brunswick House Cafe

A trip back in time

The roundabout system near Vauxhall Bridge is not a place you'd normally expect to want to linger. Waves of traffic sweep around you and huge buildings such as St George Wharf Tower dwarf everything else. But all this scenery forms the backdrop for Brunswick House, an elegantly proportioned Georgian building that seems to have landed here from a different world. It is home to the architectural salvage company Lassco, and Brunswick House Cafe.

When you enter, the feeling of being transported to another place and time gets even stronger. The building is stuffed with antiques: fireplaces, mirrors, shop fittings, and ornaments. The restaurant / cafe seamlessly merges with all this. In the cafe section, you can sit in front of beautiful old bookcases, and in the restaurant, customers dine amidst marble statues under Dutch chandeliers and flags.

Jackson Boxer and his brother Frank opened Brunswick House Cafe in 2010. They grew up in the area and Jackson had always loved this building. Frank had previously run a successful rooftop cafe in Peckham and together they approached Lassco with the idea of renting a corner of the storage annex and turning it into a coffee house. They started with a £1000 each, a coffee machine, two fridges, and a menu of soups and sandwiches. Today they offer full restaurant service for up to 200 people, including breakfast and lunch.

All the meat comes directly from small farms, fish is sourced from day-boat fishermen, and they grow some of the vegetables on a farm in West Sussex. Although food takes center stage here, they also serve excellent coffee, provided by the small south London roaster Jack Coleman, who buys beans on a small scale from plantations and roasts a bespoke seasonal blend for them. With all this Jackson has managed to achieve his goal at Brunswick House: "to set the scene for our guests to have a magical time."

Address 30 Wandsworth Road, SW8 2LG, Tel +44(0)2077202926, info@brunswickhouse.co, www.brunswickhouse.co | **Getting there** Victoria Line, Stop Vauxhall | **Hours** Mon–Fri 9.30am–12am, Sat 10am–12am, Sun 10am–5pm | **Tip** From Vauxhall Bridge you can walk along the Thames to Tower Bridge and beyond – with many interesting sights along the way.

15 Buenos Aires Café & Delicatessen

An Argentinian empire

"Imagine streets with Parisian-style buildings and mansard roofs, cafes, and Spanish voices … that's what you would see in Buenos Aires and that's what we wanted to recreate here." Kate Vargas owns Buenos Aires Café & Delicatessen with her husband Reinaldo, who is from Argentina but also carries an Italian passport.

The food and drinks offered in the cafe echo this mixture of cultures. They use suppliers from Argentina, Italy, France, Spain, and Britain, and sell a selection of Argentinian wines and beers in the deli, which they also serve in the cafe. The coffee comes from a roaster at London Bridge. Different artisan bakers provide the cakes, such as carrot and Victoria sponge. Kate constantly samples different creations to be sure she's providing the best selection of cakes possible. They also serve cheese, meat, and antipasti platters with grilled vegetables, and you can order open or toasted sandwiches with a choice of up to three ingredients. Empanadas are the signature dish of the cafe and come with fillings such as spinach and goat cheese or cheese and ham. "We sell hundreds but nobody ever seems to get tired of eating them," says Kate. The menu and atmosphere here attracts many locals, as well as lovers of Argentinian food and culture from all over London.

For years Kate and Reinaldo competed professionally on the global dance circuit and their favourite style was the tango. They eventually had to retire due to health reasons. Kate went into fashion and retail and Rainaldo became a successful *paparazzo* – his celebrity photographs on the walls bear testimony to these years. In 2005, they finally both turned their back on their second careers and together launched their third, opening a cafe. Their Blackheath restaurant followed in 2007, and 2015 saw the opening of another restaurant and cafe on 15 Nelson Road in Greenwich.

Address 86 Royal Hill, SE 10 8RT, Tel +44(0)2084886764, contact@buenosairescafe.co.uk, www.buenosairescafe.co.uk | **Getting there** Docklands Light Railway (DLR), Stop Greenwich | **Hours** Mon–Sat 8am–6pm, Sun 9am–6pm | **Tip** In nearby Greenwich Market you'll find many quaint little shops and stalls selling antiques and handicrafts.

16__ Cable Café

From cappuccino to cocktails

It could be Paris, or perhaps Brussels, in the 1940s. The ceiling is painted with dark blue oil paint and the walls are decorated with old photographs, maps, and neon signs. Just imagine Edith Piaf, sitting at the table next to you, or Hercules Poirot, lifting his hat and swinging his walking stick before withdrawing to a corner to hide behind his newspaper. This little coffee shop and bar, however, is on Brixton Road near Oval in London. The same ingenious people who own Scooter Caffé in Waterloo opened it in 2011. There's actually been a cafe on this site for more than 100 years. Named for the cable car running past its door, it used to be a classic greasy spoon, which counted the tramway staff as regular customers.

Its transformation into a vintage coffee shop/bar has definitely added to its charm. Cable Café shares several similarities with its sister on Lower Marsh, such as its eclectic, mismatched furniture. If you've already visited Scooter Caffé, you will immediately recognise owner Craig O'Dwyer's personal trademark: the beautiful old coffee machines and grinders (which he repairs himself).

The atmosphere here is different, however: more continental and slightly Art Deco. Maybe it's the live jazz and swing music played every Tuesday night, with groups and artists such as tenor saxophonist Ruben Fox, Peter Horsfall and His Quartet, and the Joe Downard Quartet. On jazz nights it gets crowded, hot, and sticky, and everyone has a great time. They also offer a selection of wines, ciders, beers, and cocktails.

During the day Cable Café serves coffee roasted by Craig that the customers praise as much as the delicious hot chocolate. Here, cake is the only food on the menu – but it's lovely and homemade in Craig and his wife Natalie's own little bakery. The changing selection includes scones, red velvet cake, lemon cake, and chocolate muffins filled with custard.

Address 8 Brixton Road, SW9 6BU, Tel +44(0)2086179629 | Getting there
Northern Line, Stop Oval | Hours Mon–Thur 8.30am–11pm, Fri–Sat 8.30am–1am,
Sun 8.30am–11pm | Tip Catch an international cricket match at the Oval Cricket
Ground!

17__Café Vintage

Tassels and roses

Walk along residential Mountgrove Road and you will unexpectedly come across Café Vintage, a charming little coffee-shop-*cum*-vintage-boutique in Finsbury Park. The imaginative window displays change according to the season. Take a seat in this lovely old–fashioned room with its patterned wallpaper, tasselled lampshades, and antique crockery, and relax, close your eyes, and imagine yourself in a different era – anytime between the 1940s and 1980s, actually. Open your eyes and choose a matching dress from the selection of vintage clothing in the back room. Try on some of the shoes and accessories as well. Now you're perfectly attired to have your coffee and cake here. There's also a small selection of vintage gifts, toys, and jewellery.

The cafe was set up in 2010 by sisters Aysha Sparks and Nadia Allman, who wanted to combine their love of baking with their love of fashion. It took many hours of toiling and lots of improvisation before it all came together behind this light blue façade in Finsbury Park.

In addition to the clothes, the cafe offers delicious breakfasts, lunches, and cakes. Granola, scrambled eggs, beans on toast with cheese, or Belgian waffles in the morning will give you fuel for the day. For lunch you can choose from among panini and toasts, sandwiches, and jacket potatoes served with salads. A special soup is also available. They use organic artisanal breads, which they sell in the shop. The cakes are excellent; there is homemade mocha cake, cinnamon bites, red velvet cake, or chocolate-chip shortbread. The fair-trade coffee is provided by Coffeeplant and there's also a nice selection of loose-leaf tea.

This is a real neighbourhood cafe and come summer you can sit outside among the locals. Until then, enjoy the tassels and porcelain roses hanging from the vintage chandelier and dream of bygone times.

Address 88 Mountgrove Road, N5 2LT, Tel +44(0)7903875750, aysha@cafevintage.co.uk, www.cafevintage.co.uk | Getting there Piccadilly and Victoria Line, Stop Finsbury Park | Hours Mon–Fri 8am–6pm, Sat 9am–6pm, Sun 10am–5pm | Tip Clissold Park features an adventure playground, paddling pool, and a mini zoo with deer, goats, butterflies, and birds.

18 Café Viva

A dream come true

Peckham is a working-class area with many diverse communities. On Rye Lane, its main shopping street, you can buy food from every country in the world. And when you're done with your purchases, stop in for a coffee at Café Viva on Choumert Street.

This friendly shop opened in 2012. Lily Gorlin, a textiles graduate from Goldsmith College, worked in cafes and restaurants from a young age and always dreamt of owning her own place. When she was ready to open Café Viva, which she named after her mother, Viv, she went looking for a good coffee roaster and found it in Volcano Coffee Works. The Volcano team not only supplied the shop with coffee but also helped Lily train her staff. The shop serves Volcano's Full Steam espresso blend and also offers weekly filter coffee options as well as a variety of teas from Teapigs.

Patrons include locals who use the cafe as a place to work, families, and students who come from the adult education centre across the road during their breaks. They love the amazing breakfast "baps" – soft bread rolls that come with veggie, bacon, and chorizo options. Nearly everything here is made on-site or comes from local suppliers. For Lily, it's not just about the coffee. "Independent businesses like mine can support each other and all feed into the local economy."

Changing lunch specials, which are advertised on the blackboard, complement the breakfast options on the menu. The cakes are made in-house and include some that are gluten free, such as the carrot, mango, and coconut cakes. In winter, the focus is on stews and soups, and in spring and summer, it's on salads. During the warmer months, they receive a weekly vegetable delivery from a community garden in Burgess Park. Another hit is the warm banana bread, with yoghurt, honey, and cinnamon piled on top. According to Lily, people get hooked once they've tried it. "I must have baked hundreds since we opened."

Address 44 Choumert Road, SE 15 4SE, Tel +44(0)2076392922, cafevivapeckham@gmail.com, www.cafeviva.co.uk | Getting there London Overground, Stop Peckham Rye | Hours Tue – Fri 7.30am – 5pm, Sat – Sun 9am – 5pm | Tip Find your favourite among the international food stores on Rye Lane, ranging from Kashmir Halal to African Food.

19__Camden Coffee House

The sweet spot

Sunni (Sunash Parekh) started his coffee career with a journey to New Zealand in 2008. He travelled around the country for three months and came to love the Kiwi coffee culture. He was curious to learn more and went on to visit coffee and tea estates in Kenya. When he returned to his birthplace in Camden, he took the leap and opened his own specialty coffee shop – Camden Coffee House – in 2009. He also met Dale Harris from Has Bean, a small roaster in Stafford, and their close collaboration eventually led to the creation of special exclusive blends.

In the years that followed, Sunni opened other cafes, in Croyden, Balham, Ladbroke Grove, and Shepherds Bush. Here in the Camden branch, the resident barista explains that the grinder plays a crucial role in achieving good coffee. Depending on how coarse or fine he sets it, he will get a different amount of coffee in the basket. That, in turn, determines the extraction time; if it's too long, the coffee burns. A skilled barista can make the same beans taste three different ways just by adjusting the grinder: "It's exactly like cooking, like a recipe for a cake." Temperature and humidity also play a role.

Sunni also founded the Camden Tea Company and blends his own range of herbal and black teas, which are available at the cafe. If you're having trouble deciding between coffee and tea, just order a "Dirty Chai," which is a chai tea latte with a short espresso. The brunch and lunch menus range from bagels and jacket potatoes to sandwiches and toasts, not to mention cakes and pastries.

Among its customers the cafe counts coffee aficionados as well as folks who just want their morning pick-me-up – but one thing is for sure: once you experience a finely brewed coffee you can't go back. When a new blend comes in it always takes about 30 to 45 minutes for the barista to find that sweet spot on the grinder. But good coffee is worth the wait!

Address 30 Camden Road, NW1 9DP, Tel +44(0)2074289477,
enquiries@camdencoffeehouse.co.uk, www.camdencoffeehouse.co.uk |
Getting there Northern Line, Stop Camden Town | Hours Mon–Fri 7am–6pm,
Sat 8.30am–5pm, Sun 10.30am–4pm | Tip Jump aboard the Jenny Wren for
a canal cruise (1.5-hour round trips from Walker's Quay).

20__Candella Tea Room

Where angels look down on you

With its murals, angels, and chandeliers, Candella is a little gem. Admittedly, it's more of a tearoom than a coffee shop, but if you enjoy having a good cup of coffee or tea while sitting in a lovely, old–fashioned cafe, you shouldn't miss this spot.

The owner, Emma Aladay, was a civil engineer in her former life. She made her dream come true when she opened Candella Tea Room in 2012. She spotted the location while driving around one day, and immediately called the owner and rented the shop. The floral murals and frescoed ceiling were handpainted by a previous owner who was an antiques dealer. After he moved out, the premises were occupied by a run-down coffee shop. It took Emma one and a half years to turn the space into what she wanted it to be.

She also put a lot of thought in the tea and coffee she serves. About 100 different kinds of tea from five different companies are on offer here, including blends Emma makes herself. The selection ranges from Speculoos to Masala Chai and Black Caramel. Emma chose her coffees with equal care, using blends from South America, India, and Italy after running a taste test with her customers. Her speciality is a classic afternoon tea with scones, clotted cream, jam, and homemade finger sandwiches. The cakes are made either by a friend who is a professional baker or by Emma herself. Her signature cake, with clementines and almonds, is called Emma's Cake. "It is very moist, but also very healthy because it contains no butter."

For Emma, the most rewarding part of her job is meeting customers and forging new friendships with many of them – like the two students from Imperial College who practically lived in the cafe for months preparing for their exams, or the couple from Canada who visited twice and then sent her a gift box of vintage crockery they had collected for years. Who doesn't love a cafe where angels look down on you?

Address 34 Kensington Church Street, W8 4HA, Tel +44(0)2079374161, candellakensington@gmail.com, www.candellatearoom.com | **Getting there** Circle and District Line, Stop High Street Kensington | **Hours** Mon–Sun 8am–7.30pm | **Tip** Pay a visit to the Serpentine Gallery in Kensington Garden. It hosts world-class contemporary art exhibitions.

21_ Chairs & Coffee

Ready to roast

Chairs & Coffee in Fulham is filled with – you guessed it – chairs. As in any other cafe, they stand around tables, but here, quite a few hang on the walls too. Do the owners just want to be prepared for a huge crowd, or is there more to it?

Simone Guerini Rocco and Roberto D'Alessandro, two friends from Northern Italy, founded Chairs & Coffee. Roberto grew up in his family's coffee shop in Verona. In 2006, he and Simone met at a restaurant in London. He returned to Italy to start his own cafe in 2008, while Simone went to Central America to work on coffee farms and at coffee-exporting companies. In 2012 they reconnected again in London, and decided to combine their knowledge and open a coffee shop together.

The food is a mixture of Italian, Australian, French, and English influences. "We make what we feel comfortable with." They bake their own chocolate and Guinness cake, carrot cake, and banana bread. For breakfast they offer scrambled eggs with an Italian twist, adding Parma ham and truffle olive oil or Italian flatbreads with rocket and cheese. In the evenings they turn the lights down and the music up and serve wine with French cheeses and Italian charcuterie platters. They also give wine-tasting classes.

The coffee, of course, is very important to Simone and Roberto. So far, they've used beans roasted by Union, Square Mile, Alchemy, and Volcano Coffee Works – always as fresh as possible. Now they have also started roasting themselves and are very excited to be experimenting with single origins and blends. Simone roasted coffee back in Italy, but traditionally, Italian beans are done much darker than in the UK. A lighter roast can enhance the flavour and brings out the subtleties of the beans.

And what about the chairs? "People always look for a deep meaning, but it was just two friends having fun!"

Address 512 Fulham Road, SW6 5NJ, Tel +44(0)2070181913, chairsandcoffee@outlook.com, www.chairsandcoffee.co.uk | Getting there District line, Stop Fulham Broadway | Hours Tue–Wed 8am–6pm, Thur–Fri 8am–11pm, Sat–Sun 9am–6pm | Tip The Roca London Gallery (Station Court) is an interesting futuristic building designed by Zaha Hadid. It hosts exhibitions, events, and meetings.

22 __ Chinwag
A labour of love

Would you like to have breakfast in a phone booth and use the loo at No. 10 Downing Street? Well, at Chinwag you can do both. You access the coffee shop through an iconic red telephone box door and the entrance to the toilet inside is an exact replica of the front door of the PM's residence. Once you're here, make yourself comfortable and have a good "chinwag" – an old English term for gossip.

This cafe, with its London-themed touches and other quirky details – such as the light made from an old shower unit and the bicycle-spoke chandelier – was started in 2013 by Eren Sukur and his partner Ellie Davis. It literally grew out of their love – as well as hard work and determination. Eren, who came to England 11 years ago, was ready to return to Turkey until he met Ellie. In the end, their fathers joined forces and helped them finance the cafe.

The shop had previously been a fast-food venue and Ellie and Eren had to invest a lot of sweat equity and imagination to transform it into what it is today. Eren is the chef and his specialty is burgers, "as big as your face, unless your face is really, really, really vast." He makes beef, lamb, chicken, and veggie varieties, all of which can be topped with a selection of extras. They also serve wraps and offer a complete breakfast menu with omelettes, eggs, and all the trimmings.

The coffee here comes from local roaster Volcano Coffee Works. In the evenings they also serve wine and other drinks. Since Chinwag is opposite Goldsmith University the cafe is packed with students during the week; on the weekends it's more relaxed and neighbourhood residents come for breakfast. It's particularly nice to sit in front of the cafe on sunny days and watch the passers-by. So whenever you're in need of a ginormous burger, a hearty breakfast, or just a good coffee, don't hesitate to stop in and enjoy this labour of love!

Address 21 Lewisham Way, SE 14 6PP, www.twitter.com/chinwagnewcross | Getting there London Overground, Stop New Cross | Hours Mon–Sat 10am–10pm, Sun 10am–5pm | Tip Walk to Deptford Market (Deptford High Street), for a broad mix of fresh fish, foods, groceries, antiques, and second-hand clothes.

23___Chriskitch

Who's the boss?

In this cafe in Muswell Hill, it's all about the food. Christian (Chris) Honor, the owner, chef, dishwasher, busser, and barista often begins his day in the kitchen at 3am, just because he loves it. Chris has been cooking professionally for 26 years. Before starting his own business he worked for Gordon Ramsay as an executive chef in the Mayfair Hotel in London and in other Grand Hotels around the world. Chriskitch is a melting pot of all his culinary experiences and passions.

Though coffee may not be the shop's main draw, it's still excellent quality. As Chris lives locally and is committed to supporting other neighborhood businesses, he sources his beans from W. Martyn, a fourth-generation roaster in Muswell Hill.

There is no fixed menu and the food is cooked fresh on the premises every day. Entering the cafe, you are immediately confronted with a beautiful display of enticing and colourful dishes as well as a selection of amazing cakes. How can you choose between a salad of asparagus, chamomile tea, orange zest, and crumbled boiled egg, and a flourless cherry-and-yoghurt polenta cake? It's too difficult, really – best to take both! The main dishes are no less popular: there are frittatas, squid, beef tongue, dried mango roasted pork loin, and more.

Chris uses all his international experience working in Michelin-star restaurants and brings it to an accessible level at very affordable prices. No wonder the cafe attracts not only locals, but diners from all over London during lunchtime. Catering services for private events are available as well.

A cookbook with Chris's favorite recipes has been published, and although he wants to open one or two more cafes, this is still a family-run business. Frequently, his young daughter keeps him company in the kitchen, plies him with blueberries, and helps him garnish the soups. Chris happily admits, "She is the boss!"

Address 7a Tetherdown, N10 1ND, Tel +44(0)2084110051, www.chriskitch.com | Getting there Northern Line, Stop East Finchley | Hours Mon–Fri 9am–6pm, Sat–Sun 10am–5pm | Tip Take a twirl at Alexandra Palace ice–skating rink (open throughout the year, Alexandra Palace Way).

24__Climpson & Sons
Coffee pioneers

Climpson & Sons is one of the pioneers of the London coffee revolution. It all started with a humble market stall in the early 2000s, and today they roast around three tons of coffee a week for cafes all over the city as well as their ever-growing online business. "The good thing," says the manager of Climpson's cafe, "is that it has all grown organically."

Ian Burgess, the founder of the business, purchased his first coffee roaster in 2005. He set up shop here, in an old butcher's shop called Climpson & Sons, and kept the name as a nod to the community. The beans are sourced seasonally, mostly from brokers, but they also have a few "direct trade coffees" through their established links to growers. Before a new blend or single origin is sold, they will usually roast a sample batch at the roastery, send it over, and everyone working here will taste it and discuss its qualities. They try to find the best recipe for each coffee and record all the feedback they receive.

Apart from espresso-based drinks, batch brew filter coffee is another favoured brewing method, and they use V60 for individual pours. The staff is both friendly and knowledgeable, and when you order an espresso drink you will be asked if you want their seasonal blend, which changes four times a year, or the beans they think are the best at the moment. Often the result will be a coffee with more interesting flavours: perhaps lighter with more fruity and acidic notes to it, such as the Fields, which has hints of green apple and toffee.

If you'd like a snack or meal to accompany your flat white or cappuccino, rest assured that everything on the breakfast/brunch menu is either homemade or locally sourced. Cakes, soups, salad, and even the bacon are house-made in the kitchen at the roastery. On Saturday there's often a long queue out the door – a testament to the quality of their offerings.

Address 67 Broadway Market, E 8 4PH, Tel +44(0)2078129829, www.climpsonandsons.com | Getting there Greater Anglia, Stop London Fields or Bus 55, Stop St Josephs Hospice (LP) | Hours Mon–Fri 7.30am–5pm, Sat 8.30am–5pm, Sun 9am–5pm | Tip Visit the Viktor Wynd Museum of Curiosities (11 Mare Street), filled with stuffed animal skins, skeletons, anomalies of nature and other bizarre objects.

25___Close-Up Film Centre
A cafe for cinephiles

With over 19,000 titles – including foreign, art house, classic, experimental, and documentary films – Close-Up is the largest independent film resource in London. It also stocks books, periodicals, and magazines relating to movies. For a small monthly membership fee you can have access to the entire library and borrow whatever you want. As an added bonus, there is also a cafe. Library members receive 10 percent off in the cafe, one guest membership card, and a discount to all the film screenings.

Close-Up is the brainchild of Damien Sanville, who opened the library on Brick Lane in 2005. He always loved movies and saw a gap in the market: there was no easy public access to film culture and history. In 2013 he moved the library to Sclater Street and created an adjacent cinema. It took a long year and a half to renovate the property and build and soundproof the 40-seat theatre, which can also screen 35-millimetre and 16-millimetre archival prints.

In summer 2015, Close-Up started showing a series of films covering the entire history of the medium, as well as movies and videos by new artists. They also offer a program of talks and events with filmmakers.

In the evenings, the cafe turns into a bar where drinks and nibbles are available before and after screenings. During the day, Musetti coffee, an Italian blend, is served. Damien chose it because he liked the strong roast and he wanted to serve something different from most other East London coffee shops. All teas served here are organic and come from Joe's Tea Company. Providence Row Bakery, a local charity that creates opportunities for homeless people, delivers their cakes. Choose from among delicious friands, carrot cake, muffins, and banana bread. Close-Up also offers savoury options such as quiche and sausage rolls. So why not become a member, have a coffee, and find your favourite movie among these vast archives?

Address 97 Sclater Street, E1 6HR, Tel +44(0)2037847970, info@closeupfilmcentre.com, www.closeupfilmcentre.com | Getting there London Overground, Stop Shoreditch High Street | Hours Mon–Sun 9am–9pm | Tip Chill out at the Old Truman Brewery (91 Brick Lane), a former brewery that now houses bars, music venues, and independent shops.

26__ Coffee Circus

Almost like strawberry jam

Coffee-starved in Crouch End? Coffee Circus, on Crouch Hill a few steps off the Broadway, is the perfect place to get your fix. This cozy little spot looks more like a living room than a coffee shop. The back is papered with old music sheets, and a lovely bird-patterned wallpaper covers a part of the front room. Local artists are encouraged to exhibit their work, and the cafe also hosts music events.

A group of friends from Lithuania opened the coffee shop in 2011, while also managing two coffee stalls at Camden Market. In 2014, they decided to concentrate only on roasting and handed over the shop to current owner, Irfan Serce. "He kept the creative and relaxing atmosphere," says head barista, Barbara. Indeed, once seated on the plush red sofa opposite the fireplace with your expertly prepared cup of coffee in hand, you'll never want to get up again.

The staff is passionate about their offerings, and they are happy to tell you all about the different coffee blends, most of which are available to purchase. Their house blend, Up Hill, by Mission Coffee Works, is made from 60 percent Mexican, 20 percent Ethiopian, and 20 percent Peruvian beans. It is quite dark in taste but lightly roasted. There is usually an espresso of the day available as well: for example, Bells, with tangerine, almond, hazelnut, and milk-chocolate notes. Apart from coffee, you can choose from a wide range of black and herbal teas by Suki Teas, with names like Mango Tango or Apple Loves Mint.

The modest food menu includes breakfast, sandwiches, soups, salads, and snacks. The cakes come from an artisan baker in Covent Garden. Regular customers sometimes stop in for coffee two or three times a day. They can also sample the various brews. Barbara particularly loves the fruitier flavours and recommends Kii AB, Kenyan beans, which they make with the AeroPress: "It almost tastes like strawberry jam!"

Address 136 Crouch Hill, N8 9DX, Tel +44(0)2083408221, info@coffeecircus.co.uk, www.coffeecircus.com | Getting there Victoria Line Stop Finsbury Park, then Bus W7 toward Muswell Hill, Stop Crouch End Broadway | Hours Mon–Fri 8am–6pm, Sat–Sun 9am–6pm | Tip Nearby, Hornsey Town Hall (the Broadway), completed in 1935, bears a slight resemblance to the Tate Modern. It was the first major modernist building in Britain.

27 _ The Coffee Room

Tastes like Italy

Until recently, Mile End was not considered a very exciting area of London to live in and was certainly not spoiled with good independent coffee shops. This is changing, however, and a great start was made when the Coffee Room opened in February 2014.

Outside there are a few seats on the pavement and a chalkboard with uplifting quotes such as, "The sun does not shine for a few trees and flowers, but for the wide world's joy." Inside, the tiny space features exposed brick walls and a recycled wood counter.

The cafe has a warm and welcoming feel but the element that will cheer you up immediately is the display of beautiful cakes and biscuits on the counter. You'll want to tuck into one of their gingerbread men or tiny cake loafs; the cannoli look amazing and there's also a selection of gluten free and vegan cakes. All the baked goods come from local VictoriaYum. Since there's no kitchen here, they've made a virtue of necessity and serve brilliant sandwiches. In addition to the classics, there's butternut, goat cheese, and honey; chicken teriyaki; and chorizo, cheese, and truffles. For winter they've reinvented the traditional caprese sandwich with brie. The coffee beans come from Climpson & Sons. Cocktails and finger food are available in the evenings.

Owners Pamela Tironi and Awet Ogbaghiorghis are both Italian. They ran a street-food market stall before this, but the cold winters were taking their toll and they wanted something more permanent, especially as they had a small child. Since this is their first cafe, they were a bit worried – but the Coffee Room quickly became a hub for the local community to meet for coffee, to chat, and to read the newspapers. This is exactly what Awet loves about it: "I prefer regulars because I know what they like, how to serve them, and what makes them smile." Visiting and local Italians alike think it tastes just like Italy here.

Address 6A Grove Road, E 35AX, Tel +44(0)2034892140, orders@the-coffeeroom.com, www.the-coffeeroom.com | Getting there Central, Circle, District, Hammersmith & City Line, Stop Mile End | Hours Mon–Wed 7am–8pm, Thur–Fri 7am–10pm, Sat 9am–10pm, Sun 9am–8pm | Tip The Ragged School Museum (46–50 Copperfield Road) displays replicas of Victorian period classrooms.

28__ Cooper & Wolf
A kanelbullar every morning

There's a little Swedish oasis overlooking Millfields Park in Clapton where you'll be greeted by freshly baked cinnamon buns (*kanelbullar*) every morning. Cooper & Wolf's warm, welcoming space is beautifully decorated with changing displays every season. There is even a small "Book Swap Shop," where you can exchange a novel for one you haven't read yet.

Stick around for lunch and try some more Swedish delicacies, such as *köttbullar*; Swedish meatballs with mashed potatoes, cream sauce, lingonberry jam, and pickled cucumber; or *fisgratäng*, a salmon fish pie in lemon-cream-dill sauce with carrots and garden pea salad. A lot of the dishes here are based on recipes Swedish co–owner Sara Ratcliffe inherited from her grandmother.

Sara is a designer who's always loved cooking. Her husband, Alex, an actor, has worked a lot in coffee shops and is very passionate about coffee. When their son was born, they decided to do something that would fit in better with their new lifestyle. They moved to Clapton and opened Cooper & Wolf in 2012. Swedish chef Paul Ivarsson developed the menu together with Sara, based on hearty home-cooked Swedish food. They pickle their own herring and cure gravlax.

Alex wanted to keep the standard of the coffee very high from day one and engaged head barista James Hamilton to look after that side of things. They use beans from Caravan roastery in King's Cross and offer a weekly selection of single-origin beans at their pour-over coffee bar. The selection of loose-leaf teas comes from Make Tea Not War.

A few years ago this area was in decline, but recently, a remarkable revival has taken place and Clapton has become fashionable again. Alex enjoys the variety of customers here. "It's not just young, trendy people. We see a lot of families with kids, runners and walkers from the park, or people who've lived locally for 30 or 40 years."

Address 145 Chatsworth Road, E 5 0LA, info@cooperandwolf.co.uk, www.cooperandwolf.co.uk | Getting there London Overground, Stop Homerton | Hours Mon–Fri 9am–5.30pm, Sat–Sun 10am–6pm | Tip Walk to Clapton Pond (Lower Clapton Road), an old village pond since the 1600s. Sit on a bench and watch the ducks!

29__Counter Café

On the water's edge

On a lovely spring or summer day, there's nothing more relaxing than a leisurely breakfast or brunch along the water's edge. One of the nicest spots you could choose for such an outing is the Counter Café in Hackney Wick. They have a spectacular pontoon on the Lea canal right next to the Olympic Park. Here you can enjoy not only a pleasant view of the waterway and Olympic Stadium, but also brilliant coffee and food.

The coffee is roasted in the cafe and all the food is prepared on the premises, a testament to the passion owners Tom and Jess Seaton have for both. The New Zealand siblings founded Counter Café in 2009 as a small local eatery. It became so popular that they moved two years later to their current location in the gallery Stour Space. They purchased an old 2.5 kilo roaster they found in someone's attic in Wales and started roasting their own coffee beans. The beans are exclusively purchased through an importer called Falcon Speciality, which shares every detail about each coffee's origin with their clients. Counter sells only single-origin roasts and offers unique coffees, often grown on micro-lots, where farmers experiment with how different varieties will react to their climate.

Apart from the regular staff, specialised chefs come to the kitchen, where they work in a separate prep area to make a particular dish or group of dishes. One such example is a local cook who comes in to make sausages with meat purchased at Smithfield Market. The sausages are paired with relishes and chutneys that are prepared according to a recipe the owner's mum developed. Many dishes on the all-day brunch menu pay tribute to Jess and Tom's family and their New Zealand heritage, including various egg dishes and their famous homemade pies, which are served with a side salad. Also popular are the homemade cakes, brownies, and chocolate-chip biscuits.

Address 7 Roach Road, E 3 2PA, Tel +44 (0)7834275920, cafe@counterproductive.co.uk, www.counterproductive.co.uk | **Getting there** London Overground, Stop Hackney Wick | **Hours** Mon–Fri 8am–5pm, Sat–Sun 9am–5pm | **Tip** Check out what's on in the Yard Theatre (Unit 2a Queen's Yard), a converted warehouse that stages challenging contemporary plays and music events.

30__Craft Coffee
A "simple" cup of coffee

Do you love chatting about coffee and want to learn more about different brewing methods? Do you appreciate having a favourite coffee spot but want to try different roasts? And most important of all: are sea salt caramel brownies your favourite? If the answer to these questions is "Yes," you'll surely enjoy a visit to Craft Coffee on Sclater Street just off Brick Lane.

In this bright cafe there are always beautiful fresh flowers on the tables. A small courtyard and a downstairs seating area offer additional space. Jamie Evans and Emily Fahey opened this shop in 2013. Before that, they sold coffee from a cart at Maltby Street Market in Bermondsey. They both bring plenty of passion and experience to the venture. Jamie worked at Bea's of Bloomsbury and Notes Coffee and Emily at Bea's and Brown's of Brockley. Having their own shop finally gave them enough scope to experiment and serve a variety of coffees suited to different tastes. They serve espresso-based coffees with organic milk from Northiam Dairy. Their roasters include Notes, Workshop, Alchemy, Caravan, Nude, Newtown, Sightglass, Tate, and others.

Jamie's favourite type is black filter coffee, freshly made with an AeroPress coffeemaker. "I'm very happy that we get more and more orders for it, because that's how a lot of the flavours come through." Every morning Jamie tests the coffee with a refractometer, a tool measuring the refraction of light shone into a substance as it sits on a lens. This is done to find out how much solid material is in the coffee in order to measure the extraction and strength of the beverage. There is an ideal amount that, for espresso, hits its sweet spot somewhere between 18 and 22 percent. In order to achieve the perfect flavour, Jamie might need to adjust the grinder, which is, of course, a Mahlkoenig EK 43. Then he'll serve you a "simple cup of coffee!"

Address 68 Sclater Street, E1 6HR, www.craft-coffee.co.uk | Getting there London Overground, Stop Shoreditch High Street | Hours Mon–Fri 8am–5pm, Sat–Sun 10am–5pm | Tip At 152–154 Bethnal Green Road you'll find Lady Dinah's Cat Emporium, a cafe with roaming cats. They don't admit customers without a booking.

31 __ Curators Coffee Gallery
Building Blocks and Magic Mushrooms

A few years ago a group of antipodeans met in London and became friends. They all loved coffee and thought investing in a specialty cafe together would be a good idea. They needed someone who could become a co–owner and run the shop for them, and they found who they were looking for in Catherine Seay, an Australian with plenty of experience. Back in Australia, she worked in chain coffee, and when she came to the UK, she was employed for several years at Kaffeine. Today she manages both Curators Coffee shops: Curators Coffee Studio on Cullum Street and Curators Coffee Gallery on Margaret Street.

Curators Coffee Studio opened near Leadenhall Market in 2012, when there weren't many specialty coffee spots. The shop is tiny and the customers are mainly office workers who come for a quick cup and a bite. In summer 2014, Curators Coffee Gallery opened in Fitzrovia with a kitchen, where sandwiches and salads are now produced for both shops. Most of their suppliers are local, as they want to support other independent businesses. The clean and simple design of both premises was brought to life by co-owner Jason Prain, who has his own furniture business.

At Curators Coffee Gallery they also have a brew bar, where single cups are made to order as well as single-estate teas from Lalani & Co. Nude Espresso roasts the signature house blend Exhibition for them. Catherine really loves coffee. She says that for her, being in the coffee business means "getting to know the craft and perfecting your skill. ... The next big thing will be experimenting with different flavours, eating with coffee or cooking with coffee. There will be a lot of innovations." Therefore, Curators Coffee has developed several "creations," such as Building Blocks, where walnut butter is mixed into the espresso and served with a cranberry juice, and Magic Mushroom, espresso served with mushroom consommé to enhance its flavour.

Address 51 Margaret Street, W1W 8SG, Tel +44(0)2075802547. contact@curatorscoffee.com, www.curatorscoffee.com | **Getting there** Bakerloo, Central and Victoria Line, Stop Oxford Circus | **Hours** Mon–Fri 7.30am–6.30pm, Sat–Sun 9am–6pm | **Tip** The recently refurbished Regent Street Cinema (309 Regent Street), birthplace of British cinema, was reopened as a working movie theatre in 2015.

32__Curio Cabal

What's in a name?

It's unclear what *Curio Cabal* means. Could it refer to fascinating objects and people who are united in a plot? According to the barista, one of the founders of the cafe, Matt Broughton, came up with the name because of its interesting associations. It all started when a group of friends who had just left university took a lease on a house and turned it into flats: "At the beginning, it was a big party house but slowly they grew up and created the co–working space and the café," explains the barista.

The workspace is called Creative Blocks and occupies the same building as the coffee shop, which opened in July 2013. There is a lovingly planted garden in the front, which is used for pop-ups, plant sales, Christmas markets, cocktail nights, etc. The cafe also doubles as a gallery for changing art exhibitions.

But even without the art, the breakfast and brunch are worth the trip. The bagel with egg and cress and the ricotta, salsa verde, and radicchio on toast are very popular. And on weekends the menu also includes dishes such as granola with raspberry and rhubarb compote, kedgeree with basmati rice, and smoked mackerel and a soft duck egg. Cakes are by Victoria Yum.

The cafe serves a medium-to-dark espresso blend from Monmouth. The guest coffee is from Guatemala by South London roaster Alchemy. If you are lactose intolerant, the barista will make you a brilliant almond milk flat white – a drink for which they are renowned.

You may wonder about the avocado plants with names on the pots that are lined up on the windowsill. It's a quirky "recycling" project. So many avocados are used in the kitchen that everyone who works here grows their own seed. Only one of them is looking a bit sad. These plants also solve the mystery of the name: Curio Cabal clearly refers to a group of baristas united to grow avocados, which take fifteen years to bear fruit!

Address 258 Kingsland Road, E 8 4DG, Tel +44(0)2072544945, hello@curiocabal.co.uk, www.twitter.com/curiocabal | Getting there London Overground, Stop Haggerston | Hours Mon–Fri 8am–6pm, Sat 9am–7pm, Sun 10am–5pm | Tip Go for a walk on the peaceful and charming towpath of nearby Regent's Canal.

33_Damson & Co

All things British

To find a relaxed space amidst the hustle and bustle of Soho isn't easy. But Damson & Co definitely fits the bill *and* serves double duty, as a coffee shop by day and a cocktail bar by night. Antonio Cardoso and Sax Arshab opened Damson & Co. in May 2013. They both wanted a British concept, and focus on procuring the best regional ingredients. They source from different farms and suppliers around the UK, beginning with the Empire espresso blend from Ozone, a local roaster. It's a medium-to-dark roast with notes of milk chocolate and fruit that's well-suited to milk-based drinks. In the summer, they produce their own cold brew with roughly ground single-origin beans. They also use an AeroPress and offer a different single origin every month.

The main focus here is on the brunch menu, which includes eggs and a range of delicious salads, freshly made in the kitchen. There are standards, such as the smoked haddock and spiced potato salad, as well as constantly changing new creations. You can order toasties and cakes during the day and a great variety of British cheeses including Ticklemore, Montgomery Cheddar, Cornish Yarg, or Colston Basset Stilton. Their charcuterie is all–British as well, so you'll be able to try forest pig-cured lomo, smoked mutton, or wild boar chorizo. The local culinary theme continues with fresh fish by Chanel Fisheries, oysters, and other seafood. In the evenings, they offer around 25 varieties of gin, British wine, vodkas, and whiskies.

Customers here are mostly neighbourhood residents or media people from nearby small production companies. "This is one of the nicest places I've ever worked," says the manager. "You wouldn't think so, but this is a close-knit community. We get a lot of couples on dates and people who bring their mum and dad." And why not? With good coffee, British cheese, and gin, it's the perfect place to invite your parents!

Address 21 Brewer Street, W1F 0RL, Tel +44(0)2036972499, social@dam
www.facebook.com/DamsonandCo | **Getting there** Bakerloo and Picca
Piccadilly Circus Opening | **Hours** Mon–Sat 8.30am–11pm, Sun 10am–
Golden Square was built according to plans by Christopher Wren. The statue in
either represents George II or Charles II and is said to have been accidentally won at
auction.

34__Department of Coffee and Social Affairs

Social entrepreneurs

Are you exhausted after hours of shopping on Oxford Street? Want to recharge with a good cup of coffee and a bite? Look no further than the Carnaby Street outpost of Department of Coffee and Social Affairs.

This cafe resides in Lowndes Court, an alley just off the crowded shopping avenue. Inside, it's spacious and light with a large basement area where patrons can gather and coffee machines and equipment are sold. Best of all, the friendly staff will make you a very good cup of coffee. CEO Ashley Lopez explains that the cafe sources single-estate beans, which are then roasted by Phil Grey. The names and descriptions are a bit more inventive than usual. There's the Stargazer espresso, which will inspire you to "… lift your eyes towards the heavens through layers of red plums and cherries, rhubarb, almonds, port wine and frangipane …" And their filter coffee, Diplomatic Corps, will "… pull the carpet out from beneath your feet in a blink of an eye." If those don't lift your spirit there are many others to either try in the shop or order from their website. Pair your coffee with a choice of sandwiches such as roast beef and Stilton or Chorizo and avocado. If you have a sweet tooth, try a slice of the honey, banana, and pecan loaf.

The Department started in 2010 on Leather Lane and has eight locations in London now, each retaining its own character. To make good coffee is not the only aim, though. The second part of the cafe's name refers to the charitable causes co-owners Stefan Allesch-Taylor, Chris McKie, and Tim Ridley and their staff members are committed to supporting. They donate to the Central London Rough Sleepers Committee and Pump Aid, which works in support of safe drinking water worldwide, among other charities – showing that humanitarian work and entrepreneurial spirit are not mutually exclusive.

Address 3 Lowndes Court, W1F 7HD, Tel +44(0)74343340,
www.departmentofcoffee.com | **Getting there** Bakerloo, Central, Victoria Line,
Stop Oxford Circus | **Hours** Mon–Wed 8am–7pm, Thur–Fri 8am–8.30pm,
Sat 9.30am–8.30pm, Sun 11am–6.30pm | **Tip** Visit the Photographers' Gallery
(16–18 Ramillies Street). They have changing photographic exhibitions and a
bookshop where you can also buy camera equipment.

35_Doppio Coffee Warehouse

Espresso with a side of jazz

Even before you enter this quirky building on Kentish Town Road, the display of espresso machines, *cafetières*, and coffee accessories in the window will pique your curiosity. Inside you'll discover a two-story-high industrial-style space with beautiful arched windows in the back and a coffee bar in the front. After ordering your macchiato, you can settle down amid boxes of merchandise and sacks of coffee beans next to a large German roaster and relax to the lilt of jazz music playing in the background.

It all began in 2010, when two business partners, Carlo Colajori and Arik Waiss, had the feeling that Britain was finally ready for an "espresso revolution." Arik already had years of experience as a distributor of Danesi Caffe. They started out leasing and selling coffee machines to shops, restaurants, and businesses out of a small storage facility. They moved to the Kentish Town space and integrated a coffee bar into the warehouse to create a unique atmosphere, giving wholesale customers the opportunity to discuss their business needs over a good cup of coffee, which they also offered to the public. The concept was so successful that they opened another shop on Hanbury Street in Shoreditch.

To wholesale clients, Doppio not only provides the espresso machine and grinder, it offers round-the-clock maintenance and repair services, and supplies them with cups and saucers, barista training, and an excellent selection of top-notch beans from mostly Italian roasters, among them Danesi, Dieme Caffe, the Duke, Italian Aroma Coffee, Tonino Lamborghini, and their own Doppio label. For some of these brands, Doppio is the only UK distributor. If you're not in the coffee business, you can still buy espresso, filters, or other home-brew paraphernalia here. And if you're a jazz fan, you're really in luck – it's the only type of music played at the warehouse.

Address 177 Kentish Town Road, NW1 8PD, Tel +44(0)2072675993, info@doppiocoffee.co.uk, www.doppiocoffee.co.uk | Getting there Northern Line, Stop Kentish Town | Hours Mon–Fri 8am–6pm, Sat–Sun 9am–6pm | Tip Before or after your visit to Doppio, go for a workout at nearby Kentish Town Sports Center (Grafton Road), a refurbished Victorian bath featuring a historic swimming pool and an array of fitness equipment and services.

36___Dose Espresso
From banker to beans

A never-ending stream of office workers, bankers, and lawyers stop at this tiny coffee shop at the south-east corner of Smithfield Market for their morning coffees. Other frequent customers are Aussies and Kiwis, who come when they get homesick for a good shot. "They know what they're paying for, which is a good-quality coffee. We try to keep our standards as high as possible," says the manager of Dose.

The shop was set up by James Philips, a former banker from New Zealand. It first opened in 2009 in an even smaller space and moved to this slightly bigger location next door in 2012. Now James runs two other cafes as well: one on the Google Campus and one on Back Church Lane in Whitechapel.

Square Mile provides the beans, with Red Brick as their house blend. Other blends include Sweet Shop and guest coffees that often come from abroad. Also on the menu are coffees made with the "clever dripper," a device combining French-press-style brewing with drip brewing, and filter coffees using the AeroPress. And of course, "good coffee needs good milk"; Dose's is organically farmed in Bedfordshire. The teas on the menu are by Waterloo Tea in Cardiff; some are meant to be brewed at a specific water temperature. Apropos of water: the water in London is very hard, which causes machines to scale up quickly and the taste of the coffee to suffer. So, to prevent that, Dose uses a filter and has installed a pump system in the basement.

The main business here is coffee but there are also breakfasts, fresh sandwiches – their specialty is a BLT on bread from Seven Seeded Bakery – and a changing selection of cakes from Bittersweet Bakers. The sandwiches are made at one of their other shops and brought here every morning.

During the seven years James made artisanal coffees in Sidney and in London, he never lost track of his goal: "to create the most beautiful coffee in the city."

Address 70 Long Lane, EC1A 9EJ, Tel +44(0)2076000382, james@dose-espresso.com, www.dose-espresso.com | Getting there Circle, Hammersmith & City and Metropolitan Line, Stop Barbican | Hours Mon–Fri 7am–5pm, Sat 9am–4pm | Tip Smithfield Market is the oldest meat market in Britain. There has been a livestock market on the site for more than 800 years. Nowadays, Smithfield deals in meat and poultry on a wholesale basis.

37 _ EC1 Coffee House

Back to the roots

There are loads of good coffee shops in Clerkenwell. But that doesn't worry Daniel Novi, owner of EC1 Coffee House. "Competition is good for us," he says, "because people have so many choices, they now understand more about coffee and know exactly what they want."

Daniel and his wife Elif opened the cafe on Clerkenwell Road in summer 2014. A large counter made of rough-hewn wood dominates the small space. It displays a variety of goods: wraps, filled croissants, granola, quiches, cake slices, pastries, and Italian cannoli. All the pastries come from a local baker. Daniel's espresso is from Allpress, a roaster from New Zealand that opened in neighbouring Shoreditch in 2010. Daniel used to work in a friend's coffee shop in South London where he sampled numerous blends – and his Italian background fuels his preference for a smooth coffee without too much acidity. Once he tasted the Allpress blend, with its notes of caramel and nuts, he knew he had to have it for his cafe.

Apart from coffee, Daniel serves a selection of teas from Teapigs, juices, and "lovey" smoothies with names such as Baby Love (strawberry, banana, and apple), I Think I Love You (banana, yoghurt, oats, honey), and Love Hangover (spinach, mint, mango, apple). Their breakfast offerings include artisan toast, porridge, eggs Benedict, and American pancakes. Elif makes a spinach cake and other Turkish recipes, including stews and soups. They plan to add more Mediterranean dishes, since the workers from the surrounding offices who come here for lunch appear to favour them.

Opening EC1 Coffee House marks a return to Daniel's childhood roots. Ten years ago, his parents managed a sandwich bar in the very same location. They owned this shop and the one next door, but later sold both properties. Daniel had his very first job here when he was 16. Now, he's back; only this time, he's the boss.

Address 45–47 Clerkenwell Road, EC1M 5RS | Getting there Metropolitan, Hammersmith & City Lines, Stop Farringdon | Hours Mon–Fri 7am–7pm | Tip The nearby Charterhouse (Charterhouse Square) is a beautiful former Carthusian monastery founded in 1371. It is still used as an almshouse (a home for gentlemen pensioners) and opens for pre-booked guided tours. The stunning garden can be seen once a year under the National Gardens Scheme.

38 __ The Electric Café

The last true egalitarian stronghold

Before you go inside the Electric Café, start by admiring the beautiful façade with its dark red Victorian signage and old-fashioned lettering.

Step through the door and travel back to a time when cabbies called you "guv" and full English breakfasts were eaten at Formica tables. You'll see washed-out brown and yellow wood panelling and an extensive breakfast and lunch menu with amazing prices that haven't risen in years. There's a photo of the cafe on the wall taken in the early 1930s, but friendly owner Stavros Tsoukkas thinks the shop is much older than that. It probably first opened around 1890, when the other houses here on the street were built, and was called Electric Parade.

Stavros's family has owned the place since 1978 and lived above it until 1999. He and his mother both work here and serve breakfast all day. The Big Breakfast contains eggs, bacon, bubble 'n' squeak, black pudding, fried tomatoes, and a free mug of tea. They even serve an American Diner Breakfast, with French toast, bacon, sausages, hash browns, and maple syrup. Everything is made from scratch in the kitchen behind the counter. Chips are hand cut and the bubble 'n' squeak is homemade as well, with potatoes sourced locally from British farms.

The customers here are incredibly diverse: "Builders, mums, millionaires, and substance abusers sit cheek and jowl. We are a throwback to a time when a cup of coffee wasn't a form of reverse snobbery or a fashion accessory. People were just looking for sanctuary with something hot served by someone who cares." Stavros loves his shop but has seen so many competitors close in recent years that he doesn't have much hope for the future – though he promises not to go down without a fight. So, having breakfast at the Electric Café might also mean supporting the last true egalitarian stronghold on the London high street!

Address 258 Norwood Road, SE 27 9AJ, Tel +44(0)2086703114 | **Getting there** Thameslink, Stop Tulse Hill | **Hours** Mon – Fri 7.30am – 4pm, Sat 8am – 4pm, Sun 9.30am – 1pm | **Tip** West Norwood Cemetery is one of the "Magnificent Seven" – seven cemeteries privately run in Victorian times.

39_Embassy East

Not too serious

After visiting busy Hoxton Street Market on a Saturday, where you can find everything from food to fashion, stop in for a coffee at Embassy East. It was founded in 2013 by three mates who worked together at Flat White and decided to leave to open their own business. According to Chris Coleman, one of the owners, it took them a year to find the site. "We choose Hoxton because we could afford it at the time. We didn't have much money to play with." To make the most of their limited budget, they did all the interior renovation themselves and repurposed salvaged and nontraditional materials, such as using jam jars as lamps and scaffolding boards as kitchen shelves. Co-owner Tommy Studholme designed most of the fittings. It came in handy that Tommy's uncle is a scaffolder and one of their friends works as a carpenter.

The cafe's brunch–oriented menu is simple but tasty, and includes items like sardines on toast and an open chorizo toastie with goat cheese, dukkah, and honey. Tommy makes their millionaire's bread and Chris's girlfriend bakes the banana bread. The brilliant coffee comes from Workshop in Clerkenwell. Having worked in coffee shops since he was a teenager, Chris, who hails from New Zealand, thinks coffee culture in London is far more advanced than it is back home. "Apart from Australia and New Zealand, the scene here is also influenced by Scandinavia. It's new and constantly evolving, and there's a strong interest in the science side of coffee." Embassy East has become a destination for coffee lovers but it is also a neighbourhood joint that draws a lot of old Hoxton locals. It's particularly busy on the weekends when the brunch crowd descends from Hoxton Street Market, so be prepared.

As they're open seven days a week, the owners spend a lot of time working here with their mates. Their recipe for success: don't be too serious!

Address 285 Hoxton Street, N1 EXQ, Tel +44(0)2077398340, info@embassyeast.co.uk, www.embassyeast.co.uk | Getting there London Overground, Stop Hoxton | Hours Mon–Fri 9am–6pm, Sat–Sun 10am–6pm | Tip Chris recommends White Lyan (153–155 Hoxton Street), a world–class cocktail bar down the road. They don't use any ice in their concoctions and the drinks are quite unusual!

40_ The Espresso Room
It's not rocket science

This small kiosk-style coffee shop opposite Great Ormond Street Hospital for children in Bloomsbury has been around for quite a while and is still going strong. It was brought to life by Ben Townsend in July 2009. Ben lived for quite a while in Melbourne, Australia, where he became obsessed with coffee, gave up his previous job, and started a career as a barista.

Back in London, he trained other baristas and worked at the London School of Coffee. In 2008, he found this space in Great Ormond Street and engaged an old friend and craftsmen, Tim Hitchens, to design the small room in a simple yet stylish way that would enable Ben and his staff to deliver the best possible quality coffee and service. Since then, the signage and interior of the cafe has somehow gained iconic status and been featured in several design magazines.

Inside there isn't much space to sit, and the square wooden benches and seats out front are occupied in nearly all weather. They sell a lot of take-away coffees to locals who live in the neighbourhood or work in the nearby hospital and surrounding colleges.

The menu is simple: a selection of cakes (try the orange and almond), pastries, and sandwiches, ranging from ham and Emmental cheese with English mustard to German sausage with sweet mustard and sauerkraut. It's undeniable, however, that coffee is the star of the show here. They use Square Mile coffee beans, as well as those from other roasters, such as Round Hill or Dark Woods. Whole beans are also available to purchase by the bag.

For Ben, good coffee is not so much about science but the mood it generates: "People in the coffee industry often make coffee for other baristas; they measure and experiment with methods and this all seems very important, but what really matters to the public is the overall experience. You don't go out to buy a science experiment. You go out to buy a coffee!"

Address 31–35 Great Ormond Street, WC1N 3HZ, Tel +44(0)7760714883, info@theespressoroom.com, www.theespressoroom.com | Getting there Piccadilly Line, Stop Russell Square | Hours Mon–Fri 7.30am–5pm | Tip Did you know that J. M. Barrie donated the royalties from his play / novel, *Peter Pan*, to Great Ormond Street Hospital – thus giving it a significant endowment?

41__Esters

For coffee aficionados

Hidden in a residential area in Stoke Newington, Esters isn't easy to find if you don't know where to look. Jack Lloyd-Jones, who co–owns the shop with his girlfriend, Nia Burr, took over the location in December 2013. Jack and Nia brought a wealth of experience to the enterprise since they'd previously worked at Fernandez and Wells and other coffee shops around London. They use mostly single-origin espressos roasted by Has Bean in Stafford and offer a new one every four weeks.

Although blends are usually served as espresso because it's easier to get the structure right, Jack likes offering single origins because they tell a story: "It's just one farmer doing one thing. You have one face behind the coffee instead of three." Their filter options are brewed with the Kalita Wave or Chemex and are changed weekly. Teas are by Postcard Teas, which sources from very small farms that the company has visited personally.

There is a modest-sized kitchen on-site where most of the food is prepared – with the exception of the croissants from Yeast Bakery and the eccles cakes and doughnuts from St John Bakery. Jack is responsible for all savoury dishes, which include sandwiches and vegetarian meals such as roasted carrots with quinoa and charred king cabbage, paprika cream cheese, and poached eggs. Nia bakes the delicious raspberry-and-almond cake as well as all the other sweets. They also make their own fresh almond milk, pickles, lemonade, granola, and jams.

Esters doesn't see many walk-ins – it's mostly regulars and coffee aficionados who frequent the cafe. Some are even owners of other specialty coffee shops who live nearby. Jack loves it because he gets to know his customers really well. One almost gave birth in the shop: while enjoying her coffee she suddenly stood up and announced, "I'm in labour!"

Address 55 Kynaston Road, N16 0EB, Tel +44(0)2072540253, hello@estersn16.com, www.estersn16.com | **Getting there** Greater Anglia, Stop Stoke Newington or Rectory Road | **Hours** Tue–Fri 8am–5pm, Sat 9am–5pm, Sun 10am–4pm | **Tip** St Mary's Church (Stoke Newington Church Street) is London's only surviving Elizabethan church. It has a spooky overgrown churchyard that's fun to explore.

42__Everbean
Coffee among butterflies

Avery Row in Mayfair is among London's quirkier lanes. It follows the path of the Tyburn, one of the city's lost rivers, which once ran aboveground from Hampstead down to the Thames and is named after Henry Avery, the bricklayer responsible for this stretch of road. With its cobbled surface and bespoke shops, it evokes the feeling of small-town Italy rather than central London. It begs for a cafe where you can sit outside and have a good latte or cappuccino. Luckily, there's Everbean, an unusual coffee shop on an unusual lane.

Its rounded façade made owners Jessica and Onur Sab fall in love with the place at first sight. At that time it was a hair salon. Inspired by the local coffee culture in Melbourne where they had lived for the previous seven years, the couple wanted to open a cafe. Once they found the perfect spot, they renovated the shop with the help of a friend who is an interior designer. Every inch of space is used to give the small but beautiful two-storey room a feeling of spaciousness. One wall features an insect mural and there are mobiles with metal butterflies hanging from the ceiling.

For Jessica, it's important that her customers feel relaxed: "Our working day consists of helping other people to get away from their working day." They serve Climpson & Sons coffee, homemade carrot cake, lemon drizzle, and banana-walnut cake; they mix hot smoked salmon or goat-cheese salad with broccoli, pomegranate, and walnut. The chef comes in at night and prepares all the food that is served the following day.

This area is like its own little village; many shops have been here for years and the local business people frequently enjoy their lunch at Everbean. If you have been shopping on Bond Street, take a break and savour your coffee here in the sunshine. And if it's raining? Pull up a chair inside and watch the butterflies dance.

Address 30 Avery Row W1K 4BB, Tel +44(0)7572615440,
www.facebook.com/pages/Everbean/202877253105185?sk=info | **Getting there** Central
and Jubilee Line, Stop Bond Street | **Hours** Mon–Fri 7.30am–5pm, Sat 9.30am–5.30pm |
Tip While shopping on New Bond Street, take a moment to look above the entrance of the
auction house Sotheby's (34–35 New Bond Street) and you'll see the oldest outdoor statue
in London: the lion goddess Sekhmet, dated around 1320 B.C.

43 — Exmouth Coffee Company

There's no sign of it

Right next to Whitechapel Gallery is a coffee shop with no name over the door and no sign in the window. The window display, however, beckons you in with its delicious cakes, pastries, and colourful salads. Usually there's also a queue out the door, especially on the weekends. If you manage to squeeze in, you'll find yourself in a narrow space with long common tables. The walls are mostly covered with white tube tiles. Take heart and wiggle through until you reach the back of the room where the open kitchen is located, separated from the rest of the cafe by a long counter. Get comfortable on one of the bar stools and watch the chefs at work.

This is Exmouth Coffee Company. It was set up by Djamal "Jam" Kabouche and Eddie Grappy in 2012. The men met in Sweet Boulangerie on Exmouth Market, a patisserie opened by Eddie in 2003. They are a good match because Jam, a passionate coffee specialist, and Eddie, chef extraordinaire, share the same culinary values.

Coffee, of course, is important at Exmouth Coffee Company, and it's not surprising that they roast their own. The medium-roast house espresso blend is a mix of beans from Brazil, Honduras, and Colombia. They use double shots for espresso-based drinks and offer single-origin drip filter coffee.

The food is a cultural mix that is all prepared on-site. In the morning you can watch the cooks making almond and chocolate croissants and flatbreads; for lunch there are pitas, quiches, and salads; and, of course, delightful cakes and meringues at any time of day. Who wouldn't queue up? The customers are a wild assortment, ranging from gallery goers, Brick Lane tourists, and locals from the surrounding Pakistani and Bangladeshi communities, to teachers and architects.

What of the mystery of the missing name? It was just so busy from day one that they never got around to putting up a sign!

Address 83 Whitechapel High Street, E 1 7QX, Tel +44(0)2073771010, exmouthcoffee@gmail.com, www.exmouthcoffee.co.uk | **Getting there** Circle, District and Hammersmith & City Line, Stop Aldgate East | **Hours** Mon–Sun 7am–8pm | **Tip** Opposite the coffee shop, Altab Ali Park commemorates the death of Altab Ali, a clothing worker, who was murdered by three teenage boys in 1978.

44__ Fernandez & Wells

A tale of two friends

Rick Wells, a British journalist who worked for the BBC, and Jorge Fernandez, a manager for Monmouth Coffee in Central London, once met – you guessed it – over a cup of coffee. Wells said, "I really like wine." Fernandez replied, "I really like coffee, but I also love cured meat from Spain." Wells countered, "I've been in France and they have very nice cheeses there." He added thoughtfully, "I'm about to retire and probably get bored." Fernandez replied, "We should put all these items together and open a business: Fernandez & Wells."

This is the story of Fernandez & Wells as told by the manager of their Beak Street shop. Is it possible that beverages other than coffee were involved? Probably. Be that as it may, the business became immensely successful and today they have six coffee shops, all over London. Beak Street was one of their first, and is popular among the locals for breakfast and lunch.

The small, cosy shop is dominated by a long counter piled high with delicious-looking cakes, sandwiches, and croissants. They serve meat boards featuring charcuterie from Spain and other countries – jamón, Parma ham, chorizo, black pudding, and morcilla – and cheese boards, with goat cheese, brebis, and Comte sourced from France, Italy, and Switzerland. To accompany these platters, there's a careful selection of wines and sherries. Cheeses and cured meats are also used in sandwiches and grilled sourdough toasts that are topped with either Spanish black pudding, morcilla, and aioli; or heritage tomatoes, garlic, and sea salt.

Fernandez is responsible for the coffee and selects the espresso blend. He chooses the beans, which are then roasted by Has Bean to his specifications. Fernandez and Wells claim they were inspired by the contents of a shepherd's knapsack: cured meat, cheeses, sourdough bread, cake, coffee, and wine. What a lucky shepherd!

CHICKEN
W/PANCETTA &
ROCKET
£5.75

Address 73 Beak Street, W1F 9SR, Tel +44(0)2072878124, www.fernandezandwells.com | **Getting there** Bakerloo and Piccadilly Line, Stop Piccadilly Circus | **Hours** Mon−Fri 7.30am−6pm, Sat−Sun 9am−6pm | **Tip** Venetian painter Antonio Canaletto once lived down the block, at 41 Beak Street, and tried to sell his paintings from there.

45 __ The Fields Beneath

The underside of the tracks

Combine the feeling of a small village and an urban hub and throw in exposed brickwork and Moroccan cement tiles; the noise of trains from above; inventive sandwiches, soups, and cakes; and lingering locals and waves of commuters – mash it all together and you get the Fields Beneath, named after the book of a local historian. Founded by Gavin Fernback and a partner in 2012, Gavin now runs the shop on his own. He has a wealth of experience in specialty coffee and worked in several third-wave coffee shops before purchasing a coffee cart in Primrose Hill and finally setting up the cafe under the railway station in 2012.

Gavin admits that he's made mistakes along the way: "It is a whole different experience being the owner. You just have to make it work." He pays his staff far above the minimum wage and enjoys the camaraderie of working as a team. Most his baristas didn't have a coffee background when they were hired and have been trained here from scratch. He also couldn't get by without some help from his mum and dad: his father does all the bookkeeping and his mother bakes cakes for the shop. Sandwiches are freshly made in the shop and a girl who lives in Kentish Town provides the homemade cookies. As many products as possible are sourced from London-based companies and 60 to 70 percent of the food is vegetarian. There are only two kinds of meat on offer because Gavin believes in quality over quantity. He wants to be proud of everything he sells.

The teas come from Butterworth and Son, and of course the team at the Fields Beneath is deeply passionate about the coffee they serve. Square Mile is one of Gavin's favourite London roasters but the cafe changes roasters every fortnight and also sells beans for home brewing. "If you're interested in coffee," Gavin says, "London is one of the best places in the world to be right now."

Address 52 Prince of Wales Road, NW5 3NL, Tel +44(0)2074248838, twitter.com/FieldsBeneath | **Getting there** London Overground, Stop Kentish Town West | **Hours** Mon–Fri 7am–4pm, Sat 8am–5pm, Sun 9am–5pm | **Tip** On Thursdays or Saturdays, visit Queen's Crescent Market, one of the oldest street markets in London where food, clothes and household goods are sold (9 minutes' walk from the Fields Beneath).

46___Fingers Crossed

Make your own luck

Have you always had a secret desire to visit North Stoke Newington, but never had a specific reason to go? Now you do. Lunch at Fingers Cross is definitely worth a special trip. This cafe offers a unique mixture of Australian and Italian food, bearing the stamp of owner Ania Weksler.

Ania comes from Australia, where she worked in several coffee shops before deciding to start her own business. She opened the cafe in December 2013. Because it was her first shop, she wanted a lucky name and chose Fingers Crossed. When she started refurbishing the premises, which previously housed a burger bar called Amhurst Griddle, she discovered old wood panelling painted in a beautiful patchwork of pastel colours. She decided to leave everything as it was and just made little adjustments. There's even a small square of the original wallpaper with a brick-and-vine leaf pattern.

Ania then hired an Italian chef who'd previously worked in the restaurant Boca di Lupo. There's no such thing as an Australian-influenced cafe without eggs, so the breakfast and brunch menu includes several egg dishes, ranging from scrambled to poached, served with caponata or chorizo. The ricotta hotcakes can be ordered savoury or sweet, and a breakfast trifle with toasted mixed nuts and grains, yoghurt, and fruit compote is one of the more popular options – as well as the quail risotto and the ham hock.

The cafe is busiest at lunchtime when they offer freshly prepared specials, which usually include a lovely pasta dish such as linguine with mussels and tiger prawns, a soup, a salad, a fish of the day, and a meat dish such as rib-eye steak, leg of lamb, or roast pork loin. Finish your meal off with a delicious piece of cake, baked by Ania, and an espresso, made with beans roasted by Has Bean. No wonder that so many of East London's creative crowds find their way here around midday.

Address 247 Amhurst Road, N16 7UN, Tel +44(0)7599842154, fingerscrossedcafe@gmail.com, www.facebook.com/fingerscrossedcafe | **Getting there** Greater Anglia, Stop Rectory Road | **Hours** Mon–Fri 8am–5pm, Sat 8.30am–5pm, Sun 10am–5pm | **Tip** Hackney Downs Studios (17 Amhurst Terrace), is an artists' community with workspaces, creative businesses, and a Sunday market.

47 __ Fix 126

Only in London

It seems like everyone in the neighbourhood drops by at least once a day to have a coffee at Fix. It's the English equivalent of the Neapolitan coffee bar, where you'd stop in front of the cafe with your Vespa running while you guzzle a quick espresso. There aren't actually are any scooters parked on the pavement here – but the energy is the same.

Fix 126 is always full of people chatting with one another or talking on their smartphones. Inside, you have all the ingredients of a London third-wave coffee shop: pressed wood tables, hardwood floors, exposed brickwork, and a wavy-blue-patterned wall. The owner, Sasha Rainey, opened his first Fix on Whitecross Street a few years ago after the cafe he was working for went bankrupt. Fix 126 is his second coffee shop. Sofie, the French manager, had overseen professional kitchens before she started here, but had no previous experience in the coffee business. She learned quickly and is now as passionate about coffee as the rest of the team. "The coffee culture here is very unique. This could have never happened in Paris. There are a lot of good coffee shops in London now and the competition is fierce, but there is a great vibe."

Fix sources coffee from London roaster Climpson & Sons. The special Fix Blend contains 50 percent Oromia Sidamo, from Ethiopia; 25 percent Suarez Colombia; and 25 percent Daterra Estate, from Brazil. They also offer guest blends, purchase their produce from local businesses, and try to avoid big brands. You can get refreshing fruit smoothies or grab a sandwich or panini from the fridge and let the staff heat it up for you. A separate kitchen supplies both shops.

At certain hours of the day it gets very crowded here: everyone in the vicinity seems to want their coffee "fix" at the same time. Which might be the reason Sasha thinks London's still in the early stage of its coffee renaissance. "It can only get better."

Address 126 Curtain Road EC2A 3PJ, Tel +44(0)2077397829, www.fix-coffee.co.uk | Getting there Northern Line, Stop Old Street | Hours Mon–Fri 7am–7pm, Sat–Sun 8am–7pm | Tip Iniva (1 Rivington Place), the Institute of International Visual Arts, creates and hosts changing exhibitions, which explore the diversity of today's society.

48_ Flat Cap Coffee

The people's choice

Only steps from Westminster Abbey, in an area full of tall office buildings, Strutton Ground Market comes as a real surprise. You suddenly find yourself on an old-fashioned cobbled lane among stalls selling food, clothing, footwear, jewellery, and, of course, coffee. For a really good cup, Flat Cap is definitely the place to go. Not only do you get a mean flat white, espresso, or latte here, but baristas Alfie and Charlie will invariably cheer you up with their friendly banter.

Flat Cap uses Notes espresso beans, which are roasted much lighter – even for specialty coffee – than the beans you'll find in most other places, which allows the more delicate flavours to come through. Notes sources their beans in different places, usually through direct trade. The coffee blend at Flat Cap is changed nearly every week. Workers from the surrounding offices that queue in front of the stall at lunchtime appreciate its quality.

Alfie, who has worked here since 2012, is used to being outside. He enjoys that customers from all walks of life stop at the stall – not just the "cool" crowd that frequents the coffee shops. He's worked at several cafes but prefers making coffee at the market: "There are no barriers. It's being a barista in its purest form. We get all sorts of people here and because Charlie" – he nods at his fellow barista – "is a bit older, older people don't feel intimidated to buy their coffee with us." Charlie worked at Strutton Ground Market for 20 years. He had a booth selling CDs and six years ago he started working at Flat Cap.

Charlie and Alfie have fun arguing about who is in charge. Asked if they know where the name *Flat Cap* comes from, Alfie guesses, "I thought it was a cross between a flat white and a cappuccino." Charlie knows better: "When we started we gave the customers a list of possible names and that's the one they chose."

Address Strutton Ground Market, Strutton Ground, SW1P 2HR, Tel +44(0)7861425172 | Getting there Circle and District Line, Stop St James's Park | Hours Mon–Sat 8am–4.30pm | Tip Tate Britain (Millbank) is not far and displays British artists such as Turner and Constable.

49__Flat White

A damn strong cup of coffee

Flat White has been on Berwick Street in Soho since 2005, making it a true veteran among London's third wave coffee shops. Back then, Berwick Street was a lot less gentrified than it is now. It was full of the "real life" of Soho, meaning drugs, barrow boys, and prostitutes.

Peter Hall, an Australian fund manager, opened the cafe. He runs an ethical investment fund that supports anti-whaling campaigns and the Javan rhino. Peter loved sitting in cafes and sipping flat whites – the drink originates in Australia and New Zealand and consists of a velvety milk micro-foam over espresso – but he couldn't find a decent one anywhere in the city. So he decided to import Aussie coffee culture to London.

James Guernsey, a friend of a friend who ran a beach cafe in Australia, helped set up Flat White in a former second-hand record shop. Unfortunately, he couldn't stay on, but another friend from down under, Cameron McLurie, stepped in, and it was Cameron who created the ethos of Flat White, which was: "Fantastic coffee, buzzy atmosphere, fun people, you're welcome, make yourself at home, and have really nice food as well." The cafe was frequented not only by homesick Aussies and Kiwis but also became, "the spiritual home of London's third wave coffee culture," as Laura Smith, Peter's partner and director of Flat White's sister café, Milkbar, explains.

The interior here in Berwick Street is simple and functional and so is the food. Dishes such as scrambled eggs on toast and avocado populate the breakfast/brunch menu. Pastries and cookies are also on offer, but coffee, of course, is the main event. From the Swedish roaster Drop Coffee, they sell espresso beans such as Kamiro, a delicious Rwandan roast with notes of lemon and strawberry. You can choose among two-, four-, six-, and eight-ounce coffees – but regardless of size, you'll get a damn strong cup of coffee here.

Address 17 Berwick Street W1F 0PT, Tel +44(0)2077340370, flatwhiteberwick@gmail.com, www.flatwhitesoho.co.uk | Getting there Northern Line, Stop Tottenham Court Road | Hours Mon–Fri 8am–7pm, Sat–Sun 9am–6pm | Tip Explore nearby Chinatown (Gerrard Street), where you'll find authentic Chinese shops, restaurants, and many other things to do, such as joining the festivities for Chinese New Year between January 21 and February 20.

50__The Fleet Street Press

Better than George Clooney

Once upon a time (or rather, as recently as 2012), there weren't any independent or specialty coffee shops on Fleet Street. So Dave and Andy decided to open one. Their cafe has a beautiful façade and a coffee–praising chalkboard sign bearing messages like, "I don't have a problem with caffeine, I have a problem without it ..." On the counter there is another small but very reassuring sign: "We make coffee better than George Clooney."

There are press photographs decorating the walls: the owners' collaboration with Fleet Street Photographers has resulted in changing exhibitions. When there are no empty chairs left in the long, narrow upstairs room, a seating area in the basement helps diffuse the crowds. It also serves as a meeting area. Dave is responsible for the "style" and coffee side of the business, while Andy takes charge of the "substance," or finances. Dave is originally from Italy, where he worked in restaurants. When he came to London, he began working at independent cafes and met Andy, who had a background in chain coffee and wanted to do something else. Their aim is simply to bring high-quality coffee and tea to the city. Fleet Street's house blend and decaf come from Caravan; the Press Blend changes seasonally; and the single-origin filter coffee rotates weekly. They serve five premium teas in pots and a wide range of herbal teas – try the Golden Monkey King, or Passion Fruit, Orange, and Mango.

If you're in the mood for a special treat, go for a hot chocolate from the Kokoa Collection. Fleet Street Press also serves homemade sandwiches and soups such as sweet potato, coconut, and coriander, as well as cakes and pastries. This is a business district and most customers either work in the vicinity or are students in need of a caffeine fix. For Dave, that's what it's all about: having regulars and getting to know them.

Address 3 Fleet Street, EC4Y 1AU, Tel +44(0)2075837757, info@thefleetstreetpress.com |
Getting there Circle and District Line, Stop Temple | **Hours** Mon–Fri 6.30am–6.30pm,
Sat–Sun 10am–5pm | **Tip** Nearby Temple Church (Temple) was built by the Knights
Templars and still contains the tombs of many knights.

51 Fork Deli Patisserie

Lunch in Bloomsbury

Stop in to this very busy coffee shop in Bloomsbury at lunchtime and your odds of finding an empty table are slim – but it's worth a try, because the salads, sandwiches, soups, and quiches are every bit as good as the cakes.

Matthew Mackenzie, Fork's manager and chef, has his own king-dom downstairs in the kitchen, were he bakes, cooks, and prepares everything served in the cafe above. The menu changes every Friday and the focus is on healthy, local, seasonal food. The cake selection is excellent and you can choose from among seven or eight different kinds: carrot cake, gluten-free orange and almond cake, or chocolate brownies, almond and cinnamon muffins, banana bread, viennoiserie, and fruit pastries. If you prefer a savoury treat, try the thyme scone with cream cheese and spring onion. During the winter, Matthew offers a different cupcake every day – the perfect mood lifter in gloomy weather.

Matthew started working at Fork in 2012, when owners André Avidian and Stuart Swycher needed a chef for their cafe. André runs a design company that specialises in global hospitality and Fork's space used to be his office. But when the company moved on to bigger premises, André turned the space into a coffee shop. Matthew had planned to stay just six months, but two and a half years later he's still here because he loves having such creative freedom.

Fork serves Monmouth coffee roasted a bit darker to achieve a result more consistent than you'd get with a lighter roast. The loose teas are from a Welsh company called Waterloo Tea, which also provides the stump teapots that are for sale.

During the week, customers are mostly students and staff from University College, and on the weekends, Fork gets a lot of visitors from farther afield who come for lunch in Bloomsbury, and linger over the coffee.

Address 85 Marchmont Street, WC1N 1AL, Tel +44(0)2073872860, info@forkdeli.co.uk, www.forkdeli.co.uk | **Getting there** Piccadilly Line, Stop Russell Square | **Hours** Mon–Sat 7.30am–7pm | **Tip** In Brunswick Square, check out the magnificent plane trees, which were part of the original Victorian planting.

52__Fowlds Cafe
A place to "recover"

For a long time Jack Wilkinson had his eye on the front room of Fowlds Upholstery, which was established in 1870 and has been in the hands of the same family since 1926. Today it's run by a member of the fourth generation, Bob Fowlds. Jack – who had a background in TV and film and worked as a prop designer – lived on the square and wanted to open a community cafe. Together with his friend Hanne Cole, who is head of the residents' association, he found a way to finance it without taking out any loans. They launched their own version of a Kickstarter campaign, asking neighbours who wanted a coffee shop to contribute by way of "pre-buying" their coffee.

It was a success, and once the funding was in place, they went to work finding a site. When they knocked on Bob Fowlds's door, he laughed at first: "Everyone comes in and gives me suggestions for what to do with the building." But Jack conveyed his vision, and in the end persuaded Bob to let them have the storefront. After Jack installed water and electricity and redesigned the small space, they opened in March 2014.

Since then, Fowlds Cafe has become the community hub Jack had always pictured. In the morning, customers stop in to buy a grain or sourdough loaf from Little Bread Pedlar and usually stay for breakfast, possibly porridge with berries, avocado on toast, or just a simple grapefruit half. While drinking Square Mile coffee, they can watch upholsterers Bob and Larry at work through the glass partition. If the sun is shining, lunches – be it homemade soup, sandwiches, or toasties – can be taken to the seating area outside. Some evenings the interior transforms into a bar and they serve craft beers, carefully chosen wines, whiskies, and cocktails (try the espresso martini). And once a month the cafe hosts Fowlds Feast, a candlelit supper for up to 30 adventurous diners, at a long table in the upholstery workshop.

Address 3 Addington Square, SE 5 7JZ, Tel +44(0)2034174500, info@fowldscafe.com, www.fowldscafe.com | **Getting there** Northern Line, Stop Oval | **Hours** Mon – Wed 7.30am – 5pm, Thur 7.30am – 10.30pm, Fri 7.30am – 11pm, Sat 8.30am – 5pm, Sun 9.30am – 4pm | **Tip** Explore nearby Burgess Park, with a lake, play areas, barbeques, world gardens, and a food-growing project.

53__Freestate Coffee

A daily ritual

At certain times of day you can make this popular cafe out from quite a distance because of the queue waiting to get coffee or lunch. Freestate Coffee opened here in 2013. The room is light, airy, and furnished with wooden school desks and old chairs. There are tempting salads, sandwiches, and pastries displayed on the counter, and a separate brew bar with V60 pour-over drip coffee.

For Dale Strickland, the general manager of Freestate, the cafe's success is based on a combination of good coffee and good service – which to him means offering reliably high-quality coffee without intimidating customers with a million details. The focus is on creating a homey space where people love to hang out. Many of the surrounding office workers come here in the mornings for coffee or a bite. The cafe serves wholesome breakfasts like porridge with berries and freshly roasted nuts and seeds, topped with cinnamon and manuka honey; breakfast sandwiches; and croissants. There is also a beautiful display of homemade cakes, muffins, and gluten-free brownies on the wood-clad counter. The toasts, such as "New Jersey Tuna Melt," with tuna, capers, spring onions, and paprika, are prepared daily on site.

Freestate serves a seasonal house blend by Union, which changes three times a year. In the summer, they use a lighter roast with notes of berries; in the cold season, it's a medium roast with chocolate, caramel, red fruit, and dried-raisin notes. "With our guest espresso we have fun," explains Dale. Their coffee comes from all over the world: Copenhagen, Chicago, and sometimes Panther Coffee in Miami because Tom, the owner, is American and often travels there. His other London cafe, New Row Coffee in Covent Garden, is much smaller but infused with the same passion for coffee and hospitality. "After all," says Dale, "we want people to have fun and come to the shop as part of their daily ritual."

Address 23 Southampton Row, WC1B 5HA, Tel +44(0)2079981017, greetings@freestatecoffee.co.uk, www.freestatecoffee.co.uk | **Getting there** Central and Piccadilly Line, Stop Holborn | **Hours** Mon–Fri 7am–7pm, Sat–Sun 9am–6pm | **Tip** Freestate Coffee is right next to Sicilian Avenue, one of London's first pedestrian areas. Designed by R. J. Worley in 1910, it has classical Italian features.

54__Full Stop.

What's brewing on Brick Lane

There are many coffee shops on and around Brick Lane, but this is one of the nicest – especially when afternoon fades into early evening and you want to switch from coffee to craft beer, wine, or cocktails. Just stay and lounge on one of the squashy 1950s sofas. Before Full Stop – which opened in 2011 – this was an antiques shop, and owners Rob Hursd and Pete Duggan have retained the original atmosphere: there are Formica tables, 1950s chandeliers, and fake leather benches. Like many other London cafes, this business began as a coffee cart. Pete owned a cart in West London's Church Street Market, and when Rob started working for him part-time, he fell in love with coffee. Together, they decided to open a cafe.

In the morning it is mostly quiet here, but things pick up in the afternoon as the students and tourists descend, and it gets really crowded on the weekends – especially Sundays – when Brick Lane Market is open.

The food is definitely worth sampling: there's homemade granola, organic yoghurt, and fresh fruit for breakfast; a bacon sarnie at lunchtime with Ginger Pig bacon on an E5 Bakehouse baguette; and in the evening, you can enjoy a craft beer such as Gipsy Hill Brew or one of the cider selections. Rob and Pete get their pastries, bread, and cakes from five different bakers, each with its own specialty.

Until March 2015, they used Square Mile coffee beans, but now they are very excited to be roasting their own coffee in collaboration with the Fields Beneath at Tate Roasters. Rob explains why they weigh their coffee: "At first we relied on the timer of the grinder, but weighing is much more accurate. You adjust the grinder but after making 20 coffees the amount of coffee grounds changes and you have to do it again."

Be it morning or evening at Full Stop, there's always something delicious brewing here on Brick Lane.

Address 202 Brick Lane, E 1 6SA, Tel +44(0)2077397086, info@fullstopbar.com, www.facebook.com/fullstopbar | **Getting there** London Overground, Stop Shoreditch High Street | **Hours** Mon–Tue 7.30am–7pm, Wed–Thur 7.30am–11pm, Fri 7.30am–12.30am, Sat 9am–12.30am, Sun 9am–9pm | **Tip** Try the legendary bagels from Bagel Bake (159 Brick Lane).

55__Ginger & White

Worth the wait

There are not many good independent coffee shops on Hampstead High Street and the demand is greater than the supply. So you'll often see crowds gathered around Ginger & White in Perrins Court, a small alley, just off the High Street. If it's packed inside, order your flat white, made with the Red Brick espresso blend from Square Mile, and enjoy the people watching outside while you wait. If you spot someone leaving, don't dally – grab the table before someone else swoops in.

The cafe was opened in 2009 by Tonia George and Nick and Emma Scott. All three had previous experience in the industry. Tonia was a food stylist and is the author of several cookbooks. Nick and Emma have worked in leading restaurants around the world and also ran a consultancy business for restaurateurs. When they saw the Hampstead premises they knew they had found the perfect spot. They united elements of antipodean coffee shops with British "caff," used products on offer at farmer's markets, added great cakes, and became hugely successful: "We were quickly packed with customers sipping flat whites and dunking soldiers into our soft–boiled eggs adorned with little woolly egg cosies (knitted by Tonia's mother-in-law)."

Building on their success, they opened another cafe on England's Lane, this time with an alcohol license, an extended brunch menu, and a wonderful wine list.

The menu at the Hampstead cafe will not disappoint. Order the Blythburgh free-range bacon, roasted tomato, and roasted-garlic mayonnaise on sourdough bloomer, or the fish finger, lettuce, and tartar sauce on London bloomer. Better yet, try one of the delicious cakes, ranging from amazing cupcakes in two sizes – very popular with the kids – to small lemon polenta drizzle loaves and peanut butter gateau with three layers of vanilla sponge. No wonder the locals fiercely guard their tables at this Hampstead favourite!

Address 4a–5a Perrins Court, NW3, 1QS, Tel +44(0)2074319098, infor@gingerandwhite.com, www.gingerandwhite.com | Getting there Northern Line, Stop Hampstead | Hours Mon–Fri 7.30am–5.30pm, Sat–Sun 8.30am–5.30pm | Tip The Everyman Cinema (5 Holly Bush Vale) around the corner has comfortable plush seats and shows both artsy and mainstream films.

56__H. R. Higgins

It's a social drink

H. R. Higgins was founded in 1942 by Harold Higgins. He had a passion for freshly roasted coffee and saw potential for a coffee company even though the English were known as a nation of tea drinkers. He opened roasting facilities in South Molton Street and began to sell coffee wholesale. Then, at the end of World War II, Harold took a trip to Tanzania and came across the Wachagga, a tribe that farms coffee on the slopes of Mount Kilimanjaro.

Higgins imported the Chagga coffee to Britain, where it became very popular. In the following years, his daughter Audrey and his son Tony joined the business. It was well enough known by then that even the Queen's cousin, Princess Alexandra, was a loyal customer. She recommended H. R. Higgins to the Queen, and the palace started buying coffee from them in 1973. Five years later, the Queen awarded the royal warrant to H. R. Higgins and the company became her one and only official coffee supplier.

Today, Higgins's grandson David manages the company. In 1984, they purchased a warehouse in Essex and now export coffee to America, Australia, Russia, and Japan. The shop on Duke Street opened in 1986. With its old-fashioned interior and beautiful antique coffee equipment, it looks as if it's been there forever. In the small cafe in the basement, customers can sample a medium roast, dark roast, and extra-dark roast, with varieties changing weekly. The cafe also offers fine teas and serves cakes from a small bakery in Wales.

"H. R. Higgins, despite being successful for many years, remains a small family business," emphasizes sales manager Melvin Jacob. Good coffee, good service, and consistency have always been more important than commercial expansion. Mr Jacob, who has been here for 12 years, had never tried a cup of coffee before starting the job. Upon doing so, however, he quickly became addicted: "It's a social drink and lifts your spirits up."

Address 79 Duke Street, W1K 5AS, Tel +44(0)2076293913, enquiries@hrhiggins.co.uk, www.hrhiggins.co.uk | Getting there Central and Jubilee Line, Stop Bond Street | Hours Mon–Fri 9.30am–6pm, Sat 10am–6pm | Tip Opposite H. R. Higgins you'll find the unusual raised Brown Hart Gardens, which were built on top of an electricity substation in 1905 to replace the communal garden that had previously existed at street level.

57_ The Haberdashery

The heart of the community

Do you like vintage pottery? Mismatched chairs and tables? Colourful bunting? Knitting crafts? All accompanied by delicious food and great coffee? If these questions get an enthusiastic, "Yes!" a journey to the Haberdashery in Crouch End should be on your agenda.

Just entering the place, with its patches of mismatched tiles and white and sage green wood panelling, will make you smile. In the summer, you can sit outside and enjoy the small garden. The counter is stuffed with old-fashioned sweets. On a rack next to it, green apples are juxtaposed with freshly baked bread, doughnuts, and pastries. Behind the counter, there's a beautiful collection of vintage crockery that is used to serve teas and coffees – and is also for sale. You can even buy the quirky handcrafts on display, such as the knitted teacups, doilies, and teddy bears made by the mother of one of the owners.

There's an all-day breakfast and brunch menu here. Have porridge or English breakfast in the morning accompanied by freshly squeezed juices; or burgers with feta cheese, sweet potato, mint, and beetroot, or a detox salad for lunch. If you want to indulge, try the thick Italian hot chocolate with marshmallows and an apple toffee-walnut-amaretto cake in the afternoon. The coffee is a special blend from Nude Espresso, and local merchant W. Martyn provides the tea.

Greg Vukasovic and Massimo Bergamin set up the cafe in 2009. They both came from a corporate background and wanted to create something completely different: a welcoming small-scale business with a strong community aspect. They've won several awards for their food and still do regular neighbourhood events such as "barboots" (nighttime flea markets) and host local musicians and art exhibitions in the evenings. They've subsequently opened a second coffee shop in Stoke Newington, which is quite a hit with the locals.

Address 22 Middle Lane, N8 8PL, Tel +44(0)2083428098, info@the-haberdashery.com, www.the-haberdashery.com | **Getting there** Northern Line, Stop Archway then Bus 41 to Crouch End Broadway | **Hours** Mon–Sun 9am–6pm | **Tip** Once a month the North London Vintage market opens its doors at St Mary's Parish Hall (Cranley Gardens/ Park Road). Check their website for dates: www.northlondonvintagemarket.blogspot.com.

58__HER

Slouching around in Haggerston

With its slouchy and mismatched faux-leather armchairs and sofas, Haggerston Espresso Room – HER for short – looks like a slightly neglected sixth-form common room, but with *much* better coffee. You'll want to sit here with your computer for ages, perhaps do a bit of work, sip your latte, and nibble a green macaroon. You may even be tempted to have a short nap in one of those exceedingly comfy chairs. But this relaxed, peaceful atmosphere is only one side of this cafe. Opened in December 2011 by Evan and First Brindle, HER has hosted monthly installations and exhibitions of various local artists since the beginning.

One major feature of the cafe's antipodean-influenced breakfast/brunch menu is the various incarnations and combinations of smoked salmon and eggs: salmon cream cheese on potato pancake; salmon, scrambled egg, and avocado on toast; salmon cream cheese filo tart; and a poached-egg-and-salmon stack. They also offer something called Sexy Toast, which is basically sourdough with a generous amount of cream cheese on top.

Lunch options include soups, such as mushroom-and-black-pepper; sandwiches, like baked chicken, spinach, and red onion; and satisfying salads. The sweet dishes are all lined up on a table between chairs and tables and it is very tempting to snatch one in passing. From brownies and cronuts to cupcakes and flapjacks, it is all there to seduce you.

Despite the good food, coffee is still the main attraction at HER. The seasonal house espresso blend is sourced from local roaster Climpson & Sons. They have changing guest blends, one of which is the Coffee Officina Fiori Blend, a dark roast with nutty notes and a sweet honey finish.

This is the perfect place to come with friends and kick back on the sofas for a while, even if you're not in sixth form anymore!

Address 13 Downham Road, N1 5AA, Tel +44(0)2072490880, herhaggerston@hotmail.com, www.herhaggerston.com | Getting there London Overground, Stop Haggerston | Hours Mon–Fri 7.30am–6pm, Sat 9am–6pm, Sun 9am–5pm | Tip Nearby is Draughts (337 Acton Mews), London's first board-game cafe!

59___Hubbub

Pisa Cathedral on the Isle of Dogs

The Isle of Dogs is surrounded by the River Thames on three sides. No one knows how it got its name, but there is no shortage of suggestions. Some say it came from the number of dead dogs that washed up on its banks; others that it's a corruption of the "Isle of ducks." Or maybe it was just a "dog's life" for people who had to live here.

First marshland and animal pastures, later home of vagabonds, thieves, and murderers, and today the financial hub of London, the isle also features a Victorian chapel, formerly St Paul's Presbyterian Church, built in 1859. The unusual façade is a pastiche of Pisa Cathedral. Today the building houses The Space, a performing arts and community centre, and Hubbub, a cosy cafe, restaurant, and bar. In this shop with mismatched furniture, a wood-clad ceiling, and arched windows on either end, you can get breakfast, lunch, dinner, coffee, tea, beer or wine, play board games, pull a book off the shelves and read, or sit on the outdoor benches when the weather is nice.

Make yourself comfortable and take your time here, because that's what the friendly staff, managed by David Baldwin, expects you to do. They also offer catering services and you can book the space for business lunches or parties. Choose from a variety of full English breakfasts, which are prepared with meat from John Charles Butchers – or build your own morning meal with a choice of extras. The coffee is sourced from Langdons of London, the tea from Teapigs. Hubbub is famous for its burgers, which come with different toppings and are served with fries and coleslaw. The menu changes often to reflect the seasons and they also serve lovely cakes and desserts such as toffee cheesecake and spiced apple cake. Cocktails can be accompanied by cured meat, cheese, and olive platters. You'll find no better spot to relax and recharge on the Isle of Dogs.

Address 269 Westferry Road, Isle of Dogs, E 14 3RS, Tel +44(0)2075155577, info@hubbubcafebar.com, www.hubbubcafebar.com | Getting there DLR, Stop Mudchute | Hours Mon–Wed 11am–11pm, Thur–Fri 11am–midnight, Sat 10am–midnight, Sun 10am–10.30pm | Tip Don't leave the building without checking to see what's on in The Space!

60__The Idler Academy

A multi–facetted business

Visiting the Idler Academy is like entering a private library: light blue walls, dark wooden shelves, Persian carpets, a comfortable lounger, leather poofs, old-school desks and chairs, and last but not least: lots of interesting books to read and buy. Once seated, you can just browse and follow the philosophy of the Idler Academy: "Be idle." When you want a break, step into the small garden for a slice of delicious cake and a drip coffee from Monmouth, or choose from a selection of black and herbal teas.

But reading, buying books, and drinking coffee is not all you can do here; the Idler Academy offers courses in public speaking, ukulele, singing, drawing, calligraphy, music, English grammar and punctuation, elocution, business skills, and many other subjects. They range from a one-afternoon tutorial on crochet – "Gin & Crochet – The Daisy Chain" – to a class running several weeks on how to improve your handwriting. The selection of books available to purchase is tied to the topics that are taught.

Manager Julian Mash explains that the Idler Academy grew out of *The Idler* magazine. Founded by Tom Hodgkinson and Gavin Pretor-Pinney in 1993, *The Idler* is a literary and philosophy magazine, which passed through several manifestations before becoming an online publication in 2014.

The Idler Academy bookshop and school, opened in 2011, is run by Tom; his partner Victoria Hull, who is responsible for the educational program; and commercial director Christian Dangerfield. Julian, apart from being the manager here, is also the author of *Portobello Road: Lives of a Neighbourhood*. He loves to work at the Idler Academy, enjoying the events and many interesting people and Idler fans who visit from all over the world. "The Idler Academy is many things at the same time," explains Julian, "a bookshop, cafe, and event venue. We are a multi–facetted business."

Address 81 Westbourne Park Road, W2 5QH, Tel +44(0)2072215908, mail@idler.co.uk, www.idler.co.uk | Getting there Circle and Hammersmith & City Line, Stop Westbourne Park or Royal Oak | Hours Wed–Sat 10am–6pm | Tip Check out what's going on at the Tabernacle (34–35 Powis Square), a nearby community theatre, exhibition space, and dance-studio-*cum*-restaurant located in a former church.

61 J & A Café

A secret spot

You haven't truly discovered Clerkenwell until you've patronised J & A Café in a hidden East London courtyard. Two Irish sisters, Johanna and Aoife Ledwidge, opened the cafe in 2008 in a former diamond-cutting factory. Today it comprises the cafe, bar, and first floor event space. In the summer it is lovely to sit outside in the secluded courtyard.

The cafe is a warm space with exposed brickwork and an open kitchen. In homage to the owners' roots, traditional Irish food is served: home-baked soda bread, Irish stew, and chocolate Guinness cake. Johanna and Aoife love simple, homey dishes and the idea of family life that's centred in the kitchen. They wanted to create that same feeling in the cafe.

J & A uses organic meat and local produce whenever possible. The menu includes egg dishes – such as organic Inverawe smoked salmon and scrambled eggs, omelettes, and sweet and savoury pancakes for breakfast and brunch; for lunch, sandwiches, soups and changing salads are served. From 3pm to 5pm, an assortment of teas is available, along with scones, Irish cheeses, and sandwiches.

Across the alley from the cafe, the bar has a cool green-tiled wall and a huge ceiling light. In the evening you can order from a small selection of bar food, including cheese and charcuterie boards and an "Irish Supper" with sausages, black pudding, and potato cake. The full-bodied espresso blend Archetype comes from J. Atkinson & Co in Lancaster. They also sell a variety of beers and cocktails.

The entire premises can be rented for parties and weddings. The sisters offer different special-event menus, ranging from the Picnic Buffet menu to the Canapés menu. Their honest approach to food and hospitality has made J & A very popular among East London's fashion set and despite its secreted location, it sometimes can be difficult to find a table here.

Address 1+4 Sutton Lane, EC1M 5PU, Tel +44(0)2074902992, info@jandacafe.com, www.jandacafe.com | Getting there Circle, Hammersmith & City and Metropolitan Line, Stop Farringdon | Hours Cafe: Mon–Fri 8am–6pm, Sat–Sun 9am–5pm, Bar: Wed–Fri until 11pm, Sat–Sun 9am–5pm | Tip Did you know that nearby St John's Gate once was a coffee house, run by the father of the artist William Hogarth? Today it's a museum and a wedding venue.

62__Kaffeine

Feeling better already?

The first things you see when you enter Kaffeine, on Great Titchfield Street, are the amazing-looking salads. The descriptions alone will make your mouth water: "Salmon coated in bubbleberry jelly, chicory, fresh black pepper curd, cucumber and wild sorrel," to mention just one.

When owner Peter Dore-Smith – who originally comes from Melbourne – opened Kaffeine in 2008, he wanted the food to be as important as the coffee. There were already quite a few Australian / New Zealand cafes around at the time, but most of them focused only on producing brilliant coffee. Peter had always worked in hospitality and was intent on offering the entire package to his customers. He advertised for a chef and found Jared, a creative and adventurous cook from New Zealand. Every week, Jared creates a new market-driven menu, and all the dishes are made fresh in the downstairs kitchen except for the pastries, which come from Seven Seeded bakery. Jared sources seasonal ingredients and plays around with the ratios until he gets it just right. His sandwiches, tarts, omelettes, and salads often include foraged goods, which come from a supplier called Forager or are collected by Jared himself – such as the wild cabbage from Devon (he had to slide down a very slippery slope to get it!) In 2015, Kaffeine opened its second venue, at 15 Eastcastle Street. Jared now runs the kitchen at the new space and his second in command has taken over at Great Titchfield.

But the focus on excellent food doesn't mean the coffee is neglected. Kaffeine's beans come from Square Mile and a new blend is offered each season. The baristas take great care to maintain consistent quality. For Peter, this is all part of the deal: to see his staff develop and enjoy their enthusiasm and effort. Yet there is always room to improve. His concept is: "No matter how you feel when you arrive, you feel better when you leave!"

Address 66 Great Titchfield Street, W1W 7QJ, Tel +44(0)2075806755, peter@kaffeine.co.uk, www.kaffeine.co.uk | Getting there Bakerloo, Central and Victoria Line, Stop Oxford Circus | Hours Mon–Fri 7.30am–6pm, Sat 8.30am–6pm, Sun 9am–5pm | Tip An eight-minute walk from Kaffeine is Fitzroy House (37 Fitzroy Street), showcasing the work of L. Ron Hubbard, founder of Scientology.

63__Knockbox Coffee
Espressino with love

A "knockbox" is a container with a sturdy bar in the middle, used by the barista to "knock" the spent coffee grounds out of the filter basket. It goes without saying that Knockbox Coffee has a particularly impressive one. Turkish owner Mete F. Dogrul designed it himself because he couldn't find one that was high enough. He also designed and built the chairs and tables, all with legs made from copper pipes. It took him three months to refurbish the shop before opening in May 2014.

The light and friendly cafe with its pretty arched windows and outdoor benches is perfectly located to observe the fashionably attired shoppers strolling by on Lamb's Conduit Street. Partly pedestrian, this street in Bloomsbury is full of upmarket menswear designer boutiques and other interesting stores, such Persephone Books, which features forgotten female authors. Overall, it's a much more relaxing alternative to Regent Street or Oxford Street – especially when you can enjoy very good coffee from Workshop Coffee, tea from the Rare Tea Company, or hot chocolate by the Kokoa Collection.

Knockbox's house espresso is not a blend, but Workshop's naturally processed single origin Cult of Done, from Brazil. The sandwiches are freshly made, using artisan bread by St John Bakery; pastries come from Little Bread Pedlar, and cakes from Gales. Lunch offerings change according to the seasons. In the winter they serve soups such as Tuscan tomato, and leek and potato.

The majority of customers are locals, coming in for a morning coffee or during their lunch break: lawyers, students, shop owners, and hospital workers from Great Ormond Street. On a sunny day, sit down in front of the cafe and order an "Espressino," a mixture of chocolate and coffee created by the Neapolitan barista. For manager Edi it is important that the staff enjoy working here: "When you do it with love, the taste is different."

Address 29 Lamb's Conduit Street, WC1N 3NG, www.knockboxcoffee.com | Getting there Piccadilly Line, Stop Russell Square | Hours Mon−Fri 7.30am−5pm, Sat−Sun 8am−5pm | Tip The People's Supermarket (72−76 Lamb's Conduit Street) is a community−oriented shop. The products are sourced responsibly and if you are a member you receive 20 percent off in exchange for working four hours a month.

64_Lantana

Spreading like a weed

Lantana cafe is named after a plant that originally came from Brazil. Now prevalent throughout Australia, it is regarded as a national icon there. Shelagh Ryan, Lantana's owner, sees the plant as a kind of metaphor for the cafe: "We are like a new species that's being introduced in London and we hope that our Australian brunch culture becomes a weed that takes over." It obviously was a successful introduction, because since opening in 2008, Lantana has won several awards and expanded to include two more locations, one in Shoreditch and one in Camden.

When Shelagh came from Australia to open the cafe, there weren't many good casual dining options in London. Together with her sister and her brother-in-law, she wanted to serve excellent coffee and simple, good food in a relaxed environment with great service. At first the coffee shop attracted mainly Australians and Kiwis, but nowadays it's a real mix of customers. They use Alchemy coffee roasters but have a bespoke Lantana blend. Every time the blend is changed they go down to the roasters, do some cupping, and choose the single origins that go into it.

The food is, of course, Australian, but with a fusion of Middle Eastern and Asian influences. There are Australian brunch classics such as corn fritters and smashed avocado on sourdough toast. A highlight of the evening menu is the duck burger with Asian slaw, lime, radicchio, and pickled cucumber. They prepare everything fresh in the kitchen and bake their own cakes. Takeout is also available if you'd prefer to dine at home. And if you fall in love with one of the dishes, you can find the recipe in Shelagh's cookbook, a collection of all her favourite Lantana recipes.

A mural with plants and insects dominates the cafe's back wall. It was created by the Australian artist Kat Maccloud. Look closely and you will even discover some Lantana plants among the flora.

Address 13 Charlotte Place, W1T1SN, Tel +44(0)2076373347, fitzrovia@lantanacafe.co.uk, www.lantanacafe.co.uk | **Getting there** Northern Line, Stop Goodge Street | **Hours** Mon 8am–6pm, Tue–Fri 8am–10.30pm, Sat 9am–10.30pm, Sun 9am–5pm | **Tip** Fitzrovia got its name from the historic Fitzroy Tavern (16A Charlotte Street), where a bohemian group of writers and artists used to meet in the 1930s.

65 _Le Péché Mignon

Feel French!

Should you ever wish to escape the cacophony of people and traffic on Holloway Road, just take a few steps off the main drag and step into Le Péché Mignon. This small cafe and delicatessen was one of the first independent coffee shops in Highbury and remains a charming oasis of calm in the neighbourhood.

Owners Ludovic Blind and Mairead Gallagher are both experienced cooks, having worked in many different London eateries before taking the plunge to start their own business. They finally found this space, close to where they lived at the time, and opened a French cafe and epicerie. Eight years later, Le Péché Mignon is still a firm favorite among the locals. It has a communal table where you can sit as long as you like, read the morning paper, and enjoy your Monmouth coffee expertly made by the barista using a Marzocco coffee machine.

Great coffee isn't the only thing you'll find here. As Ludo comes from Marseille and Mairead from Ireland, the food they prepare is French with an international flair. The croque monsieur is very popular and for weekend brunch, the eggs Benedict is an excellent choice; not to mention the selection of homemade mini quiches, soups, and stews. All the food is freshly made using seasonal ingredients. Occasionally a batch of sausage rolls made with free-range pork and apples comes out of the kitchen and fills the shop with an irresistible aroma. Some regulars claim the blueberry-filled custard tarts are the best in North London!

A selection of specialised, local market items is available as well. For instance, you can pick up cheese from Neals Yard Dairy or Mons Fromage, teas from Kusmi, or yoghurts from La Fermiers. They also stock a fine selection of biodynamic wines and beer from the London micro-brewery, the Kernel. An additional plus is the lovely outdoor space, which adds an entirely different dimension in the summer. So take a seat and feel French!

Address 6 Ronalds Road, Highbury, N5 1XH, Tel +44(0)76071826, feedback@lepechemignon.co.uk, www.lepechemignon.co.uk | **Getting there** Victoria Line or London Overground, Stop Highbury & Islington | **Hours** Mon–Sat 8am–6pm, Sun 8am–5pm | **Tip** For all you football fans: Arsenal's Emirates Stadium is within easy walking distance on Hornsey Road.

66__The Legal Cafe
Coffee, law, and fish

Combining a coffee shop and a law centre might sound a little unusual to you, but to Marshall Levine it made perfect sense. After taking an early retirement from his successful career as a lawyer, he realised he wasn't interested in playing golf for the next 15 years. He wanted to continue using his professional skills and had always dreamt of running a coffee shop. So, in 2007, he finally married the two and set up the Legal Cafe in Belsize Park in a former antiques shop.

Anyone who needs legal advice can simply make an appointment by phone, email, or in person. The cafe charges an hourly flat rate fee for consultations, and brings in experts for different legal issues such as divorce, commercial property, insolvency, wills, and probate (the only areas not offered are criminal and immigration law). There's also mediation available, to resolve disputes between local residents. The meeting area in the basement houses a legal library and can be rented for conferences and events. And of course, a free coffee is included with each consultation!

The cafe upstairs is worth a visit even if you have no pressing legal questions. Farid, who is manager and chef, comes from Algeria, lived in France for many years, and used to run a coffee shop on Baker Street; here, he offers a delicious mix of Italian, Indian, and French cuisines.

Farid arrives early every morning to prepare the salads and cook daily specials such as Thai Chicken Curry, Tri-Colour Sweet Pepper Soup, and Sticky Toffee Pudding. Bagels, baguettes, and panini also are freshly prepared, and when he has time he bakes a cake. There's an outside seating area on the pavement and the atmosphere is very relaxed.

If your legal issues are causing you anxiety, Farid will put you at ease with an Illy coffee and a smile. And if that doesn't help, try watching the fish in the beautiful tank. It is definitely calming.

Address 81 Haverstock Hill NW3 4SL, Tel +44(0)2075867412, info@81haverstockhill.com, www.thelegalcafe.co.uk | Getting there Northern Line, Stop Belsize Park | Hours Mon–Fri 8am–6pm, Sat–Sun 9am–5pm | Tip Check out what's on in the Roundhouse (Chalk Farm Road) – a great venue in a former Victorian railway shed – which offers live music, theatre, and ballet events.

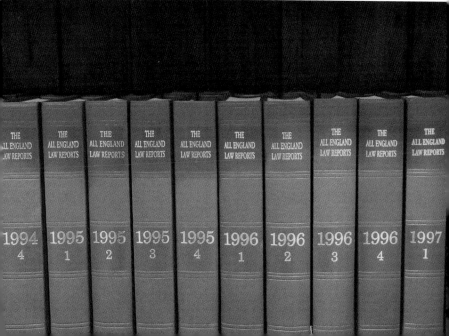

67_Lerryn's

Brunch with your mates

Lerryn's is a pretty small cafe and bar on Rye Lane, decked out in a cheery palette of peach and purple. Sandwiches here have names like Bacon Me Crazy (bacon and chilli jam on whole-meal sourdough) or Is it Dough (Jamaican sweet-bread French toast with banana and honey or bacon).

Lerryn's is owned and run by Lerryn Whitfield, who opened the cafe in April 2014 after years of working in coffee shops such as Fix, Her Haggerston, and Climpson & Sons. She has always enjoyed the cafe culture. "I identified it as one of the only ways I could make money and before I knew what I was doing, it just happened. It was all a bit of a shock and moved very quickly."

Lerryn received a lot of help from a mentor she met at Fix who encouraged her to start her own business. Before opening, she visited a number of roasters to sample their coffees but settled on Climpson & Sons because she just loved the flavor of their beans. She does cold brew in the summer and, after tasting brilliant filter coffees on a trip to New York, has plans to add some to her menu. Cakes come from two different sources: Maria at South East Cakery and Emma at Pennethorne Road.

In the evenings the cafe turns into a bar, serving cocktails and beer. Lerryn also screens films, organises different events, and often invites other chefs or street vendors to take over the kitchen and create exciting new culinary experiences. She believes she opened her cafe at just the right moment, since Peckham is in the process of gentrifying but still has a closeknit community-based core.

Lerryn enjoys creating a really welcoming atmosphere and loves having friends and locals around every day. They can bring their own records and play them in the cafe. Her shop is also known for its brunches and Bloody Marys, and nothing's better than sharing both with your mates in the garden on a sunny day.

Address 200 Rye Lane, SE 15 4NF, lerrynscafe@gmail.com, www.lerrynscafe.com |
Getting there London Overground, Stop Peckham Rye | Hours Mon–Fri 8am–6pm,
Sat 10am–6pm, Sun 10am–5pm | Tip Visit nearby Peckham Rye Park and look for the
River Peck, which comes to light for a short stretch! One of London's lost rivers, it gave
Peckham its name.

68 Lion Coffee + Records

Rockin' good coffee

On Lower Clapton Road, next to a Caribbean take-away, a small coffee shop is open for business. A wooden bench sits in front and a La Marzocco espresso machine is visible through the window. You'd never guess, however, that Courtney Love once sat on this bench and performed in the cafe.

Lion Coffee + Records belongs to Chris Hayden, the drummer in the Brit Award-winning band Florence + the Machine. The cafe was originally called Hayden Wylds but after a refurbishment, Chris reopened it under its new name in August 2014. A counter covered with wooden planks dominates the front of the shop. The beans are by the East London roaster Allpress; cakes and bread come from local bakeries. Freshly made juices, sandwiches, and rolls are available as well. In the centre of the cafe you can browse through records for sale.

The back room has a bar and is used for acoustic sessions and talks, during which cocktails and other drinks are served. Although the place is small, a lot of great events happen here. Chris wanted not only to run a coffee shop but also to have a hub for musical happenings and a meeting place for creative people. Regularly, they host gigs and acoustic sessions. Even the baristas working here are musicians; they organise events such as "Clapton Unplugged," a monthly evening which showcases local talent. The shop also hosts various author readings and exhibitions featuring works by photographers such as Bob Gruen, who is well known for his rock 'n' roll images.

It sounds like a really hip venue, but according to the barista in charge, East London creatives are not the only ones who frequent the shop. "We have an interesting cross-section of human life coming here: people from building sites popping in for a cup of tea, dog owners with their dogs, cat owners – I wish they would bring their cats! – and sometimes crazy old ladies or crazy old men."

Address 118 Lower Clapton Road, E5 0QR, Tel +44(0)2089867372, lioncoffeerecords@gmail.com, wwwLionCoffeeRecords.facebook.com/ | Getting there Greater Anglia or Bus 253, 254 towards Leman Street Stop Clapton or Millfields Road/Lower Clapton Road | Hours Mon–Sat 8.30am–5pm, Sun 10am–5pm | Tip Walk to the Round Chapel (1d Glenarm Road). Built in 1869–71 as a Congregational church, it is an extraordinary historic building, which is now a performing arts centre.

69_Lisboa Patisserie

More than just a custard tart

As the world's largest antiques fair, Portobello Market is definitely one of London's major attractions and there are many different ways to explore it. Most tourists start from Nottinghill Gate, at the south end of Portobello Road, but if you want to go about it in a way that's really relaxing, start with breakfast on Golborne Road, which crosses Portobello at its north end.

Golborne Road, overshadowed by the iconic Trellick Tower, which was designed by the architect Erno Goldfinger in 1972, is home to a strong Portuguese community; several Portuguese cafes and shops can be found here and you'll get the best custard tarts – *pastel de nata* in Portuguese – at Lisboa Patisserie. These are enjoyed by native Portuguese, celebrities, and tourists alike. Roberto, the manager, claims: "It's much more than just a custard tart." It must be, because people from all over London and beyond gather here. As soon as there is a single ray of sunshine, the pavement in front of Lisboa is crowded with people chatting, eating pastries, drinking coffee, and watching the hustle and bustle of Golborne Road Market.

Inside, the cafe is always busy but the service is fast, so you never have to wait for very long. Lisboa is a family business, headed by Carlos Gomes, who you'll find behind the till across the road at Lisboa Delicatessen. In the 28 years since Lisboa opened, it has become a local institution. Downstairs in the kitchen, they make more than 50 varieties of baked goods, many of them typical Portuguese pastries, cakes, and biscuits. Savory choices include croissants filled with Parma ham, cheese, tuna, and chicken. Another bonus is that you can get all these items on a very small budget. Don't forget to try a Portuguese coffee here. Order a *bica* – a small espresso, find a seat, relax, and when you've had your fill, head out to explore Portobello Market with renewed energy.

Address 57 Golborne Road, W10 5NR Tel +44(0)2089685242 | Getting there Circle and Hammersmith & City Line, Stop Westbourne Park | Hours Daily 7.30am–7.30pm | Tip Get your regular supply of Parma ham at Lisboa Delicatessen (54 Golborne Road). It's very good quality and very inexpensive.

70 __ The Little One

Love at first sip

Regent's Park Road at the foot of Primrose Hill is an affluent and charming neighbourhood with lots of quirky shops. It is also home to a very small coffee shop, aptly named the Little One. But for owners Lisandra and Ben Smith, the cafe was actually an *expansion* of their previous business: a white coffee van.

It all started because they felt their jobs in TV and advertising didn't give them enough time to see each other or plan a family. Both had previous experience selling coffee: Lisandra had a coffee shop back in Brazil and Ben had owned one in the UK. So they took the plunge and started the business together. As much as they loved their van, it became clear during the harsh winter of 2009 that the British climate was not conducive to an outdoor business. So they found this space, which contained an office at the time, and turned it into The Little One. Ben, who calls himself a "carpenter by trial and error," made all the shop fittings and recycled everything he could, since their budget was very limited.

Although the space here is modest, Lisandra enjoys cooking and they offer a mix of British and Brazilian dishes such as Brazilian cheese bread; blueberry, muesli, and dairy-free chocolate muffins; and their famous crepes. Coffee comes from Monmouth – because it's a favourite among the locals. In their second shop, in Camden (20 Oval Road), called The Corner One, they also offer coffee from Nude and Notes, V60 pour-over, and different guest coffees. The clientele in the two shops is quite different. They see a lot of families during the week and tourists on the weekends in Primrose Hill, while Camden's customers primarily come from the surrounding offices.

Even though they don't have much more time on their hands now than they had before, Lisandra and Ben love the freedom of owning their own businesses and not working in an office. It must be fate: they first met in a coffee shop!

WE ARE NOT SAYING FRANCHISE COFFEE SHOPS ARE EVIL... BUT WE OFTEN SEE DARTH VADER WRITING HIS SCREENPLAY IN THEM

Address 115 Regent's Park Road, NW1 8UR, Tel +44(0)7510843093
thelittleoneespresso@yahoo.co.uk | **Getting there** Northern Line, Stop Chalk
Farm | **Hours** Tue–Fri 8.30am–4.30pm, Sat 10am–5pm, Sun 10.30am–5pm |
Tip Did you know that the philosopher and co–founder of Marxist theory,
Friedrich Engels, lived at 122 Regent's Park Road?

71 London Review Cake Shop

A sweet refuge for book lovers

The London Review Bookshop, founded in 2003 by the eponymous renowned literary magazine, is a beautiful place for people who love books. But even with more than 20,000 titles to choose from, something was still missing: a place where bibliophiles could meet, talk, eat, and drink. So Terry Glover, who had previously worked with a vegan cooking collective in Australia and for Maison Blanc in London, was called in. "What I had in mind and what they wanted was kind of the same thing – so maybe it was kismet."

Terry opened the London Review Cake Shop in 2007, adjacent to the bookstore and accessible through its "history" section. Terry is inspired by her travels to Japan and Australia as well as by the seasons, and she modifies her menu accordingly. For instance, soups are served in winter, while in autumn, apples and pumpkins are prominently featured.

But there's a reason it's called a cake shop. The names alone are delectable; there's the toffee-macadamia-nut cheesecake, for instance, and the "Fifty Shades of Pink" cake that's offered on Valentine's Day. The extensive tea menu ranges from white, green, and black to herbal teas. Loose tea is provided by Jing Teas, and there's a rotation of options from Postcard Teas. Special treats are pairings such as "Autumn Leaves": chocolate cake, pumpkin ganache, and toasted almond clusters served with smoky Lapsang tea. Coffee lovers won't feel neglected either if they order the Monmouth espresso blend, a mix of Brazilian, Colombian, and Guatemalan beans.

Terry has also started combining poetry readings with afternoon teas. The liaison between book and coffee shop is still a happy one and attracts magazine subscribers, publishers, students, and book–, tea–, and coffee–lovers alike.

Address 14 Bury Place, WC1A 2JL, Tel +44(0)2072699045, bookshop@lrbbookshop.co.uk, www.londonreviewbookshop.co.uk | Getting there Central and Piccadilly Line, Stop Holborn | Hours Mon–Sat 10am–6.30pm | Tip It takes only 13 minutes to walk to the wonderful Petrie Museum of Egyptian Archaeology (Malet Place).

72 Love Walk
The best cure

Just a stone's throw from King's College Hospital, at the corner of a small road that is actually called Love Walk, is a bustling and friendly cafe with great food and even better coffee – just the right kind of place to cheer you up after an appointment at King's.

Painted brick walls in distressed white contrast with the tables made from old planks and the wood floors and counter. The walls are hung with colourful artwork, and there's a seating area downstairs with mismatched furniture and comfy old sofas. The window at the front is filled with a display of fresh, seasonal fruit, and tempting cakes and biscuits occupy the counter.

There's an extensive breakfast menu with popular dishes such as Eggs Benedict and Eggs Royale, and homemade granola and fresh fruit salad. The American Breakfast of pancakes, bacon, scrambled eggs, and maple syrup is a favourite among regulars. For something light and healthy, try a smoothie made to order, such as the Stress Beater, made with strawberries, bananas, apples, and frozen yoghurt.

Their lunch items offer something for everyone as well, ranging from panini with brie and caramelised onion, or salami, mozzarella, and roasted peppers. Other choices include sandwiches, jacket potatoes, and wraps. The dinner menu features proper meals including their famous Lasagne al Forno, served with a mixed green salad and chips. The apple pie, lemon cake, and chocolate fudge cake are all homemade. Try a slice of one with their delicious flat white, made with beans from Allpress.

The manager of the Love Walk cafe, Tony Sherisali, makes sure all ingredients are of the highest quality and uses organic produce whenever possible. The place is frequented by locals and gets very busy at lunchtime. Some of the patients at King's even look forward to going to the hospital now because they can have lunch at Love Walk afterwards!

Address 81 Denmark Hill, SE 5 8RS, Tel +44(0)2077039898, info@lovewalkcafe.co.uk, www.lovewalkcafe.co.uk | Getting there London Overground Stop, Denmark Hill | Hours Mon–Fri 7am–6.30pm, Sat 8am–6.30pm, Sun 9am–6.30pm | Tip Jazzlive at The Crypt (St Giles Church, Camberwell Church Street) is a club in a church crypt with live music, food, and cheap drinks.

73_Lowry & Baker

On the way to Portobello

If you want to have breakfast in this immensely popular little cafe on the north end of Portobello Road, you'll have to get up early – especially on weekends when the market is on. For years, this short stretch beyond Golborne Road was a neglected section of Portobello. But since the arrival of Lowry & Baker in 2010, several other cafes and independent shops have opened and the area has seen a revival.

Lowry & Baker was founded by Maya and Katie. "It was kind of an accident how it all happened," explains the manager. "Katie was working in food and Maya was doing a breakfast supper club and it just developed from there."

Once you finally find a seat in the cosy room, you won't give it up easily! You'll want to take the time to admire the collection of vintage crockery and the display of beautiful flowers from the florist next door. The counter is covered with enticing baked treats and cakes, from scones to strawberry-and-white-chocolate cheesecake. Katie and Maya try to source their ingredients, such as fruits and vegetables, from local businesses, and everything is freshly prepared. There's no separate kitchen, so the cooking is done behind the counter, and if you wait long enough, something delicious will surely come out of the oven. The breakfast or brunch menu is full of temptations. First thing in the morning could be toasted brioche or homemade granola. If more protein is needed before tackling Portobello Market, poached eggs on toast with bacon or Parma ham and avocado, or the toasted sandwich with salt beef, homemade mustard, mayo, and gherkins is equally satisfying. Enjoy your breakfast with a cup of Monmouth coffee or Teapigs tea.

Before you leave and give your table to the next person waiting, have a look at the portraits of Edith and Barbara on the wall: the grandmothers of the owners who lend their maiden names to the shop.

Address 339 Portobello Road W10 5SA, Tel +44(0)2089608534, www.lowryandbaker.com | Getting there Circle and Hammersmith & City Line, Stop Westbourne Park | Hours Mon–Sat 8am–4pm, Sun 10am–4pm | Tip Opposite Lowry & Baker you'll find Justebikes (318 Portobello Road), a brilliant shop for electric bikes.

74_M1lk

Cool beans in Balham

When you approach the quaint corner shop on Bedford Hill you will see "M1lk" written in bold pink letters across an old pub sign reading: "Almas, Real ales Take away Pub." There's also an outdoor sitting area on pedestrian Hildreth Street. M1lk, opened in 2012, is a collaboration of Julian Porter and Lauren Heaphy, both budding actors, and Lauren's stepdad, Ugur, who previously ran a Turkish cafe on the premises, which the trio decided to turn it into a specialty coffee shop.

M1lk was so successful that they opened a second cafe in the middle of Clapham Common, called Fields, in 2014. The eclectic mix of vintage items displayed on M1lk's shelves – ranging from hovering prams and Madonnas to laboratory glassware – shows Lauren's artistic background. And the cooking is as inventive as the decor. M1lk's manager explains how it works: "We look at the food from two different aspects. We do an all-day breakfast/brunch menu, but we also create three bespoke dishes every week." Creating these specials challenges the chef and entices the customers to try new things. It could be something like hibiscus kedgeree with smoked eel, fennel, katsuobushi, and soy-pickled egg, or Jerusalem artichoke soup with hazelnut oil, sherry grapes, and sourdough bread. For breakfast they offer various enticing egg dishes.

The produce is sourced from independent, family-owned suppliers around London and the south-east. The meats are organic, heritage, or rare-breed, from farms in Sussex, Norfolk, and Surrey. The coffee comes from Workshop, with Cult of Done espresso as the house blend. They also serve coffee from the renowned Swedish roaster Koppi.

Since it first opened, the cafe has become so popular that there are often long queues at lunchtime. Balham has only recently developed a bit of a "cool" status and M1lk has definitely made it even cooler.

Address 20 Bedford Hill, SW12 9RG, Tel +44(0)2087729085, julian@m1lk.co.uk, www.m1lk.co.uk | Getting there Northern Line or Southern Railway, Stop Clapham South or Balham | Hours Mon–Sat 8am–5pm, Sun 9am–5pm | Tip On Saturdays you can visit Balham Farmers Market (Chestnut Grove) before or after breakfast at M1lk.

75_Milkbar

Something that blows their mind

In Australia and New Zealand, "milkbar" is what you call the corner shop where you buy milk, cigarettes, sweets, treats, and everything else you've forgotten. It's also a place where neighbours meet and chat. London's Milkbar, a welcoming coffee shop, has become a similar hub of social activity.

Milkbar was opened in 2008 by Australian fund manager Peter Hall, who had introduced Australian coffee culture to London three years earlier with Flat White (see p. 106). Although only three minutes apart, the atmospheres in the two cafes are completely different. Flat White is more coffee-focused and 90 percent of the drinks it sells are takeaway, while customers at Milkbar tend to sit and stay awhile. Laura Smith, Hall's partner and director of the shop, explains that they don't have a traditional manager because "the idea is that everyone knows what they're doing." This is also a place where baristas stick around for years, which is unusual for the fast-moving London coffee scene.

The cafe offers a simple breakfast- and brunch-oriented menu, including eggs, bagels, and soups – and, of course, some sweets. Laura particularly recommends the caramel blondie. The espresso beans come from Square Mile, and since Milkbar was the award-winning East London roaster's first customer, they've been given their own label and attend cupping sessions at Square Mile every two to three months in order to change their single-origin coffee. Milkbar also serves Drop Coffee from Stockholm and batch brew filter coffee, as well as Sandows cold brew.

Some time ago the cafe had a bit of a down patch. Laura, although she met Peter a year after he founded Flat White, only recently became more involved in running the business and has helped revive it. She believes coffee shops are works in progress: "In the end it's all about the coffee and customers' experience: to give them something that blows their mind."

Address 3 Bateman Street, W1D 4AG, Tel +44(0)2072874796, info@milkbarsoho.co.uk, www.milkbarsoho.co.uk | Getting there Northern Line, Stop Tottenham Court Road | Hours Mon–Fri 8am–7pm, Sat–Sun 9am–6pm | Tip Check what's on at Curzon Soho (99 Shaftesbury Avenue), one of London's best art-house cinemas.

76 Moka East Café at The View Tube

A community hub

"This is the first building built for the Olympics, the place you could come and watch the whole area change," explains David Illari from Moka East Café at the View Tube. This conglomeration of vivid lime-green shipping containers is visible from afar: a stand-alone building right next to the Queen Elizabeth Olympic Park. Today it's a community centre that houses the cafe, a bike rental and repair shop, changing art exhibitions, a community garden, and classrooms for educational programs.

Before the Olympics, someone else ran the cafe and it was closed for the duration of the games for security reasons. David used to manage a coffee shop on Stratford High Street, and when he heard this site was available he thought, "Wouldn't it be fun to have a cafe in a big green shipping container?" He applied, and has been running things here since 2012.

Thanks to the bike shop, this has become a hub for cyclists: many rides start here and groups come in for coffee before or after their outings. It also attracts visitors to the park, as well as runners who are training. In the summer, patrons can enjoy barbeques in the garden, which has amazing views. Another type of event here is the "supper club," where a guest chef takes over the kitchen for an evening.

David's main coffee bean suppliers are Climpson & Sons and Union, but sometimes he uses other roasters, such as Volcano Coffee Works, Counter Café, Workshop, or Caravan. As a former set designer, David has collected a lot of things, among them all the furniture in the shop and many vintage coffeepots. He enjoys the creative parts of his job, such as making his own salt beef or baked beans for breakfasts and brunches. He sources cakes from six different bakers, but only when he thinks they'll make it better than he can!

Address The Greenway, Marshgate Lane, E 15 2PJ, Tel +44(0)7506870837, mokaeast@gmail.com, www.theviewtube.co.uk | Getting there DLR, Stop Pudding Mill Lane | Hours Mon–Sun 9am–5pm | Tip Consider renting a bike here to explore the Olympic sites.

77 Mother's Milk

Precision coffee

Mother's Milk is all about the coffee. Owners James Wise and Will Hilliard don't even bother offering anything else. The two worked in specialty coffee shops for a few years before they finally decided they'd rather work for themselves than for someone else. Mother's Milk opened in November 2013. You'll find the coffee shop inside a former sandwich bar called Rosalind's Kitchen (the old signage is still on the window). The décor is minimal, but the partners brought in their own beautiful Victoria Arduino Leva espresso machine as well as stools and other furnishings.

Because they only sell coffee, it needs to be exceptional. After lots of testing, the pair found JB Kaffee, a roaster in a small town in Germany. JB, which stands for Johannes Bayer, is a one–man operation. Schwabhausen, where he resides, was recently voted the "nicest-smelling place in Germany," presumably due to the coffee aromas. James and Will have complete trust in Bayer's taste because he only sources beans he likes. Mother's Milk offers JB's espresso and filter coffees as well the beans for purchase in the shop.

The shop attracts many customers from the surrounding offices and nearby British Broadcasting Company, as well as being a regular stop for aficionados exploring the London coffee scene. Expectations are high, so the staff weighs the coffee because – even if the amount is predetermined – grinders are never 100 percent accurate. The amount that comes out of the grinder varies because as it gets warmer later in the day, less coffee comes through. The difference can be up to five grams. Another factor is the water temperature, which should be neither too hot nor too cold. The aim is to minimize these variables to achieve consistency. Therefore the first thing Will does when he opens in the morning is to make himself some coffee. Then he adjusts the amount until he's happy with the result – and is confident his customers will be too.

Address 12 Little Portland Street W1W 8BJ, Tel +44(0)7985966275, mothersmilkcoffee@gmail.com, www.mothersmilkcoffee.com | **Getting there** Bakerloo, Central and Victoria Line, Stop Oxford Circus | **Hours** Mon – Fri 8am – 4pm | **Tip** Not far from here, BBC Broadcasting House, the BBC's worldwide headquarters (Portland Place), occupies an imposing Portland stone building. You can book a tour on the BBC website.

78__ The Nightingale
A spoonful of sugar

Near Victoria station, you won't find many snack options beyond chain coffee and pre-packed sandwiches. But if you venture a few steps further afield to Grosvenor Gardens, you'll discover the Nightingale. The little cafe resides in an old apothecary, originally founded in 1871. The former Tate Pharmacy was once a supplier to the Prince of Wales. The current owner, Pasqual, opened the coffee shop here in 2012. He kept the beautiful old interior – dark wooden shelves with inset drawers and a dispensing counter – and simply added Thonet chairs and small tables. A few apothecary jars even remain on the top shelves, which are otherwise stocked with teas, coffees, and olive oils that are for sale. A sparkling crystal chandelier floats above it all.

Once seated, you feel transported back to a time when hats and gloves were part of everyday attire. The place has a Parisian air to it, probably because Pasqual is French. Akli, the Algerian manager, was a junior sous chef for White's Gentlemen's Club, the oldest and most exclusive of its kind in London. He finds working at the cafe much more relaxing. The customers here either come from the surrounding offices or they are tourists on their way to Buckingham Palace, delighted to have a break in these lovely surroundings.

They serve coffee from Molinari with a fun twist: it comes with an edible spoon! A good selection of teas includes kusmi, jasmine, and mint. All the sandwiches are made with sourdough bread from Poilane. Popular menu choices include the pastrami sandwich, hummus, or meze dips. Akli makes the quiches, soups, and bread-and-butter pudding fresh daily in the tiny kitchen. For lunch they serve a limited menu of pasta and meats.

If you're very courageous, venture down the narrow steps into the basement: you will find that even the loo seems to have escaped the passage of time with its original Victorian tiles.

Address 39 Grosvenor Gardens, SW1W 0BD, Tel +44(0)2076300157 | Getting there Circle, District and Victoria Line, Stop Victoria | Hours Mon–Fri 7am–8pm, Sun 8am–7pm | Tip Visit the Queen's Gallery in Buckingham Palace, which shows different aspects of the Royal Collection in changing exhibitions.

79___Noble Espresso

Coffee on the go

If you're on your way in or out of town and are yearning for a quick cup of coffee, stop by Noble Espresso, located just outside King's Cross Station on Battle Bridge Place. Come rain or shine, the simple stall under the black awning is set up every morning before it opens at seven, and then packed up and taken away on a van every afternoon when it closes at four.

There is no table service or place to linger, so the focus is entirely on the quality of the cup, which is excellent. Their main house roaster is Notes, but they also serve beans from Workshop, Square Mile, and even a Berlin roaster called the Barn. Noble Espresso also sells pastries and loose tea from Joe's Tea in Hackney.

Shaun Young, the owner of the stand, lived in Australia for a couple of years but originally comes from Chester, "where you can't find good coffee." He became head barista at Kaffeine and stayed on there for two years. He loved it but was eventually ready to do his own project. Not wanting the financial risk that came with opening a cafe, he started selling coffee at festivals and smaller markets. In 2013, he was offered the stall at King's Cross, and since the rent was relatively low, he seized the opportunity.

Shaun meets a lot of interesting customers here – travellers from all over the world, but also students and office workers from the surrounding businesses and institutions. "It's vastly different than working in a coffee shop," Shaun says. "In winter it's not much fun but in the summer it's the best job in the world."

He's still not ready for his own brick-and-mortar shop, however, saying that he prefers to concentrate instead on the special-event side of his business. He provides coffee for London Fashion Week, the London Design Festival, and other happenings around the city, and has crafted a niche for himself with clients like Nike, Topshop, and Habitat.

Address Kings Cross, Battle Bridge Place, N1C 4TB, Tel +44(0)7854895078, hello@nobleespresso.com, www.nobleespresso.com | Getting there Circle, Hammersmith & City, Metropolitan, Northern, Piccadilly and Victoria Line, Stop King's Cross St Pancras | Hours Mon–Fri 7am–4pm | Tip Visit the British Library (Euston Road). Here you can read 14 million books and see changing exhibitions.

80 Ozone Coffee Roasters

The pub for modern times

Ozone Coffee Roasters in Shoreditch is very busy most days. The beautiful Leonard-Street cafe features a large concrete counter in the middle of the warehouse-type room, with tables and benches aligned along the walls. The delicious scent of coffee rises up from the roastery in the basement and will make you impatient to try the different blends. But before you order, have a look downstairs, where the 1975 PROBAT roaster takes its turns. There is a small seating area there as well.

The main blends roasted at Ozone are called Empire, Hodson, Two Trees, and Clipper. They also roast a single origin, which changes every few weeks. The company aims to establish direct relationships with coffee growers and brokers in the countries of origin. Their roasters regularly visit coffee farms to better understand the conditions and the challenges the farmers face.

Ozone was founded in 1998 by Jamie and Karen Hodson. The couple once worked with street kids in El Salvador and returned to New Zealand with the idea of establishing a closer link to the growers so that they could make more of a difference in their lives. They opened Ozone, which soon became one of New Zealand's largest provincial coffee roasters. Their legacy continued when Craig McFarlane took over in 2001. Lizzie and James Gurr, working in close collaboration with New Zealand partners Craig McFarlane and Karla Gichard, opened the London cafe in 2012.

The menu here is antipodean. Everything is seasonal and ingredients are sourced locally: fresh produce comes from Chegworth Valley, cheeses from Neil's Yard Dairy, bread from Dusty Knuckle Bakery, and bacon and sausages from Ginger Pig.

In the evenings, the cafe serves organic wines and local beers and is busier than ever. So the Ozone team may have a point when they say we should think of the coffee shop as "the pub for modern times!"

Address 11 Leonard Street, EC2A 4AQ, Tel +44(0)2074901039, info@ozonecoffee.co.uk, www.ozonecoffee.co.uk | **Getting there** Northern Line, Stop Old Street | **Hours** Mon – Fri 7.30am – 6pm, Sat – Sun 9am – 5pm | **Tip** Check out the Book Club (100 – 108 Leonard Street). It's a workspace and cafe by day, and an event space, club, and bar by night.

81 Prufrock Café

Delayed gratification

Hailed as a "mecca for coffee nerds" and an "altar of coffee," Prufrock Café on Leather Lane comes with its share of accolades. As often happens with a place so highly praised, it's tempting to search for fault, but good luck finding any here.

Prufrock was founded by Gwilym Davies, world barista champion in 2009. His partners are Jeremy Challender, a songwriter who runs the workshops and coffee diploma classes offered at the cafe, and Klaus Kuhnke, a German artisanal baker who produces all the cakes and pastries. Before Gwilym opened Prufrock, he had two coffee carts, on Whitecross Street and Columbia Road.

The focus is definitely on the coffee here, with Square Mile beans as the house blend and many different guest coffees available, including JB Kaffee from Germany. Recently they started serving filter coffee, using different elaborate brewing methods – such as coffee syphons, AeroPress, Chemex, and various Japanese techniques – to create drip coffees with brilliant results. All the coffee equipment, including espresso machines, is available for purchase. If you are addicted to espresso but don't (yet) have the skills of a barista, choose Sage, the Oracle, by Heston Blumenthal. It's a coffee machine with automatic grinding, tamping, and milk texturing. If that's beyond your budget, try out one of the classes. Prufrock offers latte art workshops, private barista training, and practice sessions.

Apart from the coffee, there are other enjoyable aspects to this shop. It occupies a generous, industrial-looking space with an eclectic collection of coffee spoons sharing the wall with more traditional art. The food's good too. Kuhnke's desserts will make your day and the salads and sandwiches come fresh from the kitchen.

The only thing one could possibly complain about is how busy it gets during the week. But it's certainly worth the delayed gratification!

PRUFROCK COFFEE

B.R.A.T CENTRE

MONDAY – FRIDAY
8AM – 6PM

SATURDAY & SUNDAY
10AM – 5PM

Address 23–25 Leather Lane, EC1N 7TE, Tel +44(0)2072420467, www.prufrockcoffee.com |
Getting there Central Line, Stop Chancery Lane | Hours Mon–Fri 8am–6pm, Sat–Sun
10am–5pm | Tip At the Craft Beer Co. Clerkenwell (82 Leather Lane) you can sample an
amazing selection of micro–brews.

82__Rapha Cycle Club
Hang up your bike!

At Rapha Cycle Club, bikes are as welcome as humans. Rather than lock up your wheels outside and risk a theft, here you can bring your bike in with you and hang it on one of the hooks provided at the front of the shop.

This clothing-shop-for-cyclists-*cum*-cafe can be found at the Regent Street end of Brewer Street. Simon, the owner of the Rapha clothing company launched in 2004, always wanted a retail space to go along with the apparel so he could demonstrate the concept behind the brand. After a successful trial with a pop-up shop, he launched the London outpost of the Rapha Cycle Club in 2012. Here, cyclists can find everything they need, from caps to jackets, T-shirts, trousers, socks, and shoes. They sell not only the classic gear needed for racing and serious cycling, but also a "city collection," comprising jeans and other everyday clothes designed with the urban biker in mind; they have reflective parts and are closely cut, hardwearing, and fast-drying.

The concept of "keeping cycling in mind" is equally applied to the food selection for the cafe. There is a "Pre-ride" menu, with lots of protein-packed items like eggs and salmon. The "On the bike" menu features high-energy brownies and granola bars, and the "Post-ride" menu is all about replenishment, with dishes like Moroccan chicken salad, smoked mackerel, and other diverse salads.

The Rapha Cycle Club has an alcohol license but is only allowed to serve beer and wine with food. Fabrique bakery in Hoxton provides the pastries and Workshop Coffee supplies the beans. You don't have to be a cyclist to enjoy the cafe here, but if you are, you'll be interested to know that the club organises several weekly rides that usually start and finish at the shop. One of them is a pre-work ride on Thursday mornings, beginning at 6:30am and returning at 8am for coffee and breakfast.

Address 85 Brewer Street W1F 9ZN, Tel +44(0)2074949831, ccldn@rapha.cc, www.pages.rapha.cc / clubs/london/club-cafe | **Getting there** Bakerloo and Piccadilly Line, Stop Piccadilly Circus | **Hours** Mon–Fri 8am–8pm, Sat 8.30am–7pm, Sun 10am–6pm | **Tip** The National Portrait Gallery (St Martin's Place) lets you experience British history through its famous paintings.

83_Regency Café
The legend

It would be hard to find a more beautiful example of a "greasy spoon" than the Regency Café in London. The black–tiled Art Deco exterior is stunning. Equally amazing is the interior, with original yellow–cream tiles, red gingham curtains, Formica tables, and a gleaming old–fashioned coffee machine. The walls are adorned with photos of boxers and Tottenham Hotspur football players. The Regency dates back to 1946 and has been featured in several films, among them *Brighton Rock* and *Layer Cake*. It's also been named by Yelp.com as one of the best restaurants in Britain. Today, the now legendary cafe is owned by Claudia Perotti and Marco Schiavetta, whose parents bought it from the original owners in 1986.

If you want a hearty English breakfast at a good price, order the "Set Breakfast Deal," which comes with bacon, sausage, eggs, beans or tomatoes, bread or toast, and tea or coffee. Extras include black pudding, bubble 'n' squeak, and hash browns. This type of breakfast is called a "fry up" because most of the ingredients are fried. Drink a "builder's tea" with it: a very strong brew served in a mug with at least two spoons of sugar. Come back later for lunch or an evening meal such as the homemade steak pie, with an outer crust of thick pastry that conceals tender meat in a tomato sauce and is served with chips, gravy, and peas. Other options are fishcakes or steak-and-kidney pudding.

Finish your English culinary experience with a delicious homemade bread-and-butter pudding. But be on alert once you order: there's no table service and Marco or Claudia will call out your dish at the top of their voice.

Customers here range from workers to businessmen and occasionally tourists who have seen the films or heard about the cafe. There's a loyal base of regulars. Many of them are familiar to the owners because they've been coming here for 25 years or longer.

Address 17–19 Regency Street, SW1P 4BY, Tel +44(0)2078216596 | Getting there Victoria Line, Stop Pimlico | Hours Mon–Fri 7am–2.30pm, 4pm–7.15pm, Sat 7am–12pm | Tip If you visit Tate Britain (Millbank), stop in to their cafe for a coffee. The Tate has its own roaster.

84__ The Roastery

A little piece of New Zealand in Clapham

The smell of freshly roasted coffee permeates the air as you approach the Roastery, on Wandsworth Road in Clapham. Follow your nose to the back of the cafe where the scent originates. The small roaster located here, called Bullet Coffee Cartel, supplies fresh beans to the shop as well as several other cafes and restaurants in the area.

The beans are roasted in small batches, so you can watch the machine at work and take your coffee home immediately. On the shop's blackboard are listed their single-origin roasts. Since coffee is seasonal, the origins vary with the time of year, coming from different countries, including Peru, Colombia, Papua New Guinea, and Guatemala. All the beans are organic and fair-trade-certified Arabica.

New Zealander Phil Ross opened the Roastery in 2009 because he found it very difficult to find a quality cup of coffee in Clapham. "I used to roast coffee in New Zealand, so it was a natural progression to start here in Clapham." They serve double shots as the standard but if you want something else they are very happy to oblige. Phil believes that "anyone can appreciate good coffee, you don't have to be an expert." He also emphasizes how important it is for the staff to be friendly and approachable.

Naturally, the food is antipodean as well, and mostly made on the premises. Dishes include corn fritters with asparagus, bacon sour cream, and sweet chilli sauce and French toast with bacon, bananas, and maple syrup; but their signature breakfast is the "Bullet Bang" – eggs and award-winning sausages from Clapham Common butcher Moens & Son. Or try the epic burger, made with a homemade beef patty, cheese, beetroot, tabbouleh, and an egg. Many of the ingredients are sourced locally.

Customers here are usually neighbourhood residents or coffee lovers who enjoy experiencing a little piece of New Zealand in Clapham.

Address 789 Wandsworth Road, SW8 3JQ, Tel +44(0)2073501961, www.bullet-coffee.com |
Getting there London Overground, Stop Wandsworth Road | **Hours** Mon–Fri 8am–5pm,
Sat–Sun 9am–5pm | **Tip** Next door to the Roastery, Puppet Planet (787 Wandsworth Road)
sells every puppet you can imagine, from glove puppets to marionettes and shadow puppets!

85 __ Scooby's Boutique Coffee Bar

Serving Puppaccinos and Dog-gestives

This is not exactly your average coffee shop. Here, dogs are not only permitted but encouraged, invited, and pampered. And that makes the eclectically furnished cafe at the end of Fortis Green Road in Muswell Hill a *must* for dog owners and their pooches. The interior is of course canine-themed; there are dog busts on the walls, a terrier doorstop, dog lamps, and dog seats. You can even buy leashes, clothes, and other accessories for man's best friend. The service counter is divided in half: one side for humans and one side for hounds.

Before opening Scooby's in 2014, owner Lisa Owen-Jones had a career in the music business and felt guilty about leaving her little dog, Florence, alone all day while she was at work, and wanted to make a change. She told herself: "If you don't give it a go, you'll never know!"

There is a whole menu just for pups provided by four professional dog bakers. Hounds can choose among "Dog-gestives" (cheese bone biscuits), "Lollypups," and "Flap Jack Russells." Lisa even makes "Puppaccinos," a canine cappuccino made with milky green tea extract, which is lapped up enthusiastically by her furry customers. Interested dogs can celebrate their birthday in the cafe or invite friends to a tea party. "I've never had a dog fight break out in here," says Lisa. "They are usually very well behaved."

But dogs are not the only ones who can get a decent cappuccino at Scooby's. The coffee for humans is from Caravan and is offered along with sandwiches and several artisan cakes, such as blueberry, honey lemon poppy, Guiness, and red velvet. Many locals feel very much at home here – with or without their pets.

The best thing about Lisa's new venture? Florence holds court most of the time and greets everyone with a friendly tail wagging.

Address 224/228 Fortis Green Road, N10 3DU, Tel +44(0)2084444693, lisa@scoobysboutique.co.uk, scoobysboutique.co.uk | **Getting there** Northern Line, Stop East Finchley | **Hours** Tue–Sun from 10am | **Tip** Are you a Kinks fan? Have a look at the childhood home of Ray and Dave Davies (6 Denmark Terrace)! Afterwards, you can have a pint at O'Neill's (87 Muswell Hill Broadway), a church converted to a pub.

86__ Scooter Caffé
Bob the cat

Craig O'Dwyer, the owner of Scooter Caffé, has a passion for machines. Being an aircraft mechanic, he first started repairing old coffeemakers – you can still see a lot of them on the top shelves in the shop – and later advanced to old scooters and cars. Scooter Caffé actually started as a boutique for vintage motorbikes in 2000, which explains the antique scooter that greets you at the front of the cafe. Scooter fans shouldn't lose faith, though: Craig still has his workshop; he just moved it to Clerkenwell.

Coming from New Zealand, a quiet little cafe was almost an inevitable part of the workshop for Craig. But it started to take over in 2009 when they got an alcohol license. Now, the cafe is open from 8:30am to 11pm and is buzzing the whole time. It still has a very relaxed atmosphere, at least partly thanks to the resident cat, Bob – who *really* owns the place. In 2011, they opened another venue, Cable Café (see p. 40), near Oval, that hosts live jazz performances every Tuesday night.

Craig and his wife like to do everything themselves: they roast their own coffee with a 1950s roasting machine from Paris, which Craig repaired himself. The coffee is from Guatemala, with tangy notes. Craig claims he still has to learn a lot about roasting, but his customers are very pleased with the results of his trials. They recently also opened a little bakery, where they prepare all the cakes for the two cafes.

Next up are plans to brew beer and make their own wine – and perhaps even brandy. Aside from the pastries, such as almond cake and cinnamon rolls, there's little for customers to purchase besides the coffee, but patrons are welcome to bring their own meals. Eventually Craig would like to have a small kitchen at Cable Café. "It's obviously more work if you're doing everything yourself," says Natalie, Craig's wife. "There are faster ways to make money, but it's very much a lifestyle thing."

Address 132 Lower Marsh, SE1 7AE, Tel +44(0)2076201421, scootercaffe@gmail.
Getting there Bakerloo Line, Stop Lambeth North | Hours Mon–Thur 8,30am–1
Fri 8.30am–12am, Fri 8.30am–1pm, Sat 10am–12am, Sun 12pm–10pm | Tip The
Florence Nightingale Museum (2 Lambeth Palace Road) explores the life and lega
of the nursing pioneer.

87 — Sharps Barber and Shop

Coffee and a shave

During their long history, both barbershops and coffee houses have become known as hotbeds for news and gossip, and as places where revolutions, conspiracies, and other plots are planned – so it's only natural to combine the two, right? That's what Sharps Barber and the design and coffee consultancy team Rob Dunne and Victor Frankowski thought when they collaborated to open this cafe on Windmill Street.

Step inside Sharps Barber and Shop and you will find the coffee shop at the front and the hairdresser at the back, separated by a large glass window. The barbershop has painted chequerboard floors and classic black and white tiles. Customers who come in for a haircut are offered free coffee. On top of the large wooden counter in the cafe and taking pride of place is "Spirit," the most beautiful espresso machine made by Kees van der Westen, which produces only a few hundred a year.

Serving good coffee is very important to the folks here. The beans used are often from Square Mile or Workshop, but there is no house blend per se, and beans are sourced from various European countries, including samples from Hungary and Poland. The aim is to offer coffee from a different country or city each month. Trying to be hospitable in the most literal sense, Sharps wants to make everyone feel comfortable. They see a coffee shop as a "mezzo sphere" between a private and a public space, with the advantages of both.

A cafe is all about ambiance, and here the vibe is so good that even the baristas fell in love with it right away: "When I got the job I was so surprised and so happy – it's the nicest coffee shop I've ever worked at." So settle in for a coffee and a pastry or an almond lemon cake, make yourself comfortable, and watch the barbers expertly wield their scissors – or better yet, have a trim yourself! The possibilities are endless.

Address 9 Windmill Street, W1T 2JF, Tel +44(0)2076368688, www.sharpsbarbers.com |
Getting there Northern or Central Line, Stop Goodge Street or Tottenham Court Road |
Hours Mon, Fri 10am–7pm, Tue, Wed, Thur 10am–8pm, Sat–Sun 11am–6pm | Tip
Are you a sucker for dresses and shoes from the 1920s to 1940s? Visit Revival Retro
(30 Windmill Street), which offers a broad range of vintage-inspired clothing.

88 __ The Ship of Adventures

The pirate way

A pirate boat has dropped anchor in Hackney between two ordinary shops on Kingsland High Street. Enter the Ship of Adventures and you'll find yourself inside a buccaneers' vessel, complete with portholes, treasure chests, and a lifeboat.

The Ship of Adventures is sailed by the Hackney Pirates, a charity charged with developing literacy and confidence in the young people of Hackney. It occupies the entire building and there's much more to see beyond the very beautiful cafe / shop at the front. Downstairs, in an amazing "underwater" space, young aspiring swashbucklers and volunteers read and write together. The children are referred here by their schools and come one afternoon per week. At the end of each term, the charity produces and publishes a booklet with all the children's works, available for purchase in the shop. They also organise holiday projects and works with older children, who have a special room dedicated to them, decorated with a South Sea mural and a huge blackboard. The rooms here can also be rented for children's birthday parties or meetings by other charity groups.

The shop and cafe first opened in spring 2014. Founded by North London teacher Catriona Maclay in 2010, Hackney Pirates got a five-year lease for the building from the council and turned it into this amazing space with the help of some designer friends. The cafe-*cum*-shop upstairs is open to the public and uses Bells espresso blend from Mission Coffee works to make drinks with names like Flat White Shark and Long Blackbeard. They also serve sandwiches, salads, soups, and brilliant cookies, all made in the tiny kitchen.

"With the profits from the cafe and shop, we would like to cover the overhead costs for staff and the building," explains Laura Marney, head of trading for the charity. The aim is to "keep growing, keep working with children, just doing it the pirate way."

DO YOU KNOW OF WAYS

TO ESCAPE BLACKBEARD'S GAZE?

Address 138 Kingsland High Street, E 8 2NS, Tel +44(0)2033271777,
ship@hackneypirates.org, www.hackneypirates.org | Getting there London Overground,
Stop Dalston Kingsland | Hours Tue–Fri 8.30am–6.30pm, Sat 11am–6pm,
Sun 12pm–6pm | Tip Bring your kids and challenge them to find the shop's
secret tunnel!

89_ Shoreditch Grind

An East London icon

Coming up from Old Street Tube Station, exit 8, you'll see Shoreditch Grind right away. It inhabits a black cylinder at Old Street Roundabout. It's just the place for a quick caffeine fix during the day – and it turns into a cocktail bar at night, when you're equally desperate for a drink.

This used to be a mobile phone shop that belonged to the father of the current owner, David Abrahamovitch. David started working in the shop when he was just 13. After his dad passed away, he inherited the failing business and a building he loved. He decided to transform it into something new and asked his friend Kaz James, a disk jockey from Melbourne, to help him. Kaz missed Australian coffee culture and agreed to help David reinvent the shop as an espresso bar on one condition: he wanted to create a recording studio in the upstairs space. That was in 2011, and the rest is history. Today the music studio is still there and Shoreditch Grind sells 500 coffees before lunchtime alone. They've added two other cafe locations, in Soho and Holborn.

It took them a while to perfect the coffee. Working together with a boutique roaster, they ultimately used reverse engineering to develop a custom blend: the "Grind & Co. House Espresso Blend" is 40 percent Honduran, 40 percent Guatemalan, and 20 percent Ethiopian.

The science of coffee is important to David and Kaz but they also aim to be accessible and not treat it all too seriously. "We're really into it," says David, "but not every customer has to be. Some just want a flat white that is better than the next flat white." They use a similarly purist approach for the cocktails: the espresso martinis contain espresso, vodka, a bit of simple syrup, and nothing more.

Although he's already planning on opening yet another shop near London Bridge, Shoreditch Grind is still David's favourite. Here is where it all began – and now it's an East London icon.

SHOREDITCH GRIND
BABY ITS COLD OUTSIDE

Address 213 Old Street, EC1V 9NR, Tel +44(0)2074907490, www.shoreditchgrind.com |
Getting there Northern Line, Stop Old Street | Hours Mon–Thur 7am–11pm,
Fri–Sat 7am–1am, Sun 9am–7pm | Tip Wesley's Chapel (49 City Road) was built in
1778 by John Wesley, the founder of Methodism. The museum tells the history of the
Methodist movement.

90__Small White Elephant
The mystery of life

Lots of plants inhabit the narrow space that is this cafe; the walls are painted in vibrant colours and works of art hang everywhere. Jennifer Richardson and Dale Carney, aka Jehn and Dale – both artists and baristas – come from Devon. They started Small White Elephant in the summer of 2014. They'd worked in the coffee world for a long time and were ready for a place of their own. "We wanted to have a cafe where we could do everything we loved under one roof." They invite local artists to put up their work and change the exhibits every three weeks. They show their own art as well, and Jehn makes the cards and jewellery that she sells in the shop. In the evenings there are poetry readings and the shop hosts a monthly jazz night – the next project is storytelling nights.

Dale and Jehn's favourite espresso blends come from Alchemy – most of the time they use Elixir but they also serve the Opus blend. They do V60 filter coffees and offer coffees from changing guest roasters such as Extract Coffee Roasters in Bristol, with really interesting flavours like Parma violets or black olive, allspice, and lavender. One of the specialities here is the Vietnamese drip coffee. It is a strong, sweet drink served with condensed milk, and takes about five minutes to drip through.

It took Jehn a long time to decide on a tea supplier. She finally found Solaris Botanists and is very happy with their clean-tasting teas. The Malaysian-style Teh Tarik tea is served with a bit of a dramatic flair, its froth produced by pouring the tea into a jug from high above. The savoury food, which includes sandwiches, is prepared in the cafe's kitchen but Jehn bakes most of the cakes off site.

Asked why the cafe is called Small White Elephant, Jehn explains: "Once I had a dream in which I solved the mystery of life. It had to do with small white elephants. I don't remember what happened, but one day I will."

Address 28 Choumert Road, SE 15 4SE, smallwhiteelephant@gmail.com, www.smallwhiteelephant.com | Getting there London Overground, Stop Peckham Rye | Hours Mon 9am–6pm, Wed–Fri 9am–6pm, Sat–Sun 10am–5.30pm | Tip For a night of clubbing, try the CLF Art Café (133 Rye Lane).

91 Soho Radio
Coffee on air

Based in the heart of Soho on Great Windmill Street is a small coffee shop that doubles as a radio station. Soho Radio was founded in April 2014. Its aim is to showcase what the neighbourhood is all about: its vibrant and diverse culture and rich history. Both residents and local industry get a voice here.

Film, television, comedy, food, and science are all represented in the station's programming, which is an eclectic mix of music and chat. There's live-streaming as well as pre-recorded content and music ranging from jazz to rap. Interviews with stars, filmmakers, chefs, and poets can also be heard on Soho Radio – with everyone from Boy George to the local piano tuner. The social problems of the area are discussed; a movie show reviews the newest cinema and DVD releases; residents voice protests against the closure of important local institutions; and in the weekly science club, an experiment is performed live on-air using ingredients from the kitchen cupboard, and guest scientists chat about their favourite songs.

The founders wanted to be acoustically at the centre of Soho's cultural life, but also physically visible so locals could actively participate. So they decided to broadcast from a shop where you can enjoy a good cup of coffee while you watch the live radio show through a large glass window. To ensure the quality of their coffee, Soho Radio collaborates with Department of Coffee and Social Affairs (see p. 76), which provides their own roasts. They also serve tea, pastries, and biscuits.

Joe Hopper usually stands behind the counter. "I'm the person that's always here." He's the face of Soho Radio and also makes a brilliant flat white. Both the radio station and the shop have had an amazing response from the local community. People believe in it and want to support the business. "They really get what we're doing," says Joe proudly.

Address 22c Great Windmill Street, W1D 7LD, Tel +44(0)2071234567,
cafe@sohoradiolondon.com, www.sohoradiolondon.com | Getting there Bakerloo
and Piccadilly Line, Stop Piccadilly Circus | Hours Mon–Fri 8.30am–5pm,
Sat 10am–5pm | Tip Just next door, at 20 Great Windmill Street (formerly the
Red Lion pub and now the lively Be At One cocktail bar), Karl Marx and
Frederick Engels submitted their proposals for writing the Communist Manifesto.

92 St David Coffee House

Three friends in between jobs

You will find St David Coffee House set back from busy David's Road on a raised terrace. This quirky little cafe with its eclectic interior near Forest Hill Station is worth the trip, especially on a Saturday morning when the farmers' market is on.

First opened in 2009, the location was taken over in 2012 by three friends: Jordan Cluroe, Russell Whitehead, and Sian Polhill-Thomas. All three are actors and wanted to have a business to work at in between jobs. Jordan and Russell also have an interior design company called 2 Lovely Gays, and are responsible for the decor of the cafe: a mixture of old and new with displays of art, vintage crockery, and old books. Sian is the manager and runs St David on a daily basis while still pursuing her theatrical career.

They take their coffee very seriously. "None of our coffees leave the kitchen without being measured and weighed," says Sian. "I'm learning more about coffee every day." They serve Red Brick from Square Mile as their house blend and use V60 and AeroPress to make filter coffee with a selection of guest roasters from the UK and Europe. They experimented with 14 different types of milk before finally settling on one from Northiam Dairy, a small farm in the Kent and Sussex Downs.

On the breakfast/brunch menu you'll find granola, egg and soldiers, and poached eggs. Seasonal toasted sandwiches are made fresh daily. On Friday and Saturday nights, St David's serves a selection of wines, craft beers, snacks, and cheese and meat boards. Sian loves interacting with their diverse customer base, which ranges from creatives and business people to market traders. "You can't just do coffee," she says. "Recently we developed an interest in street food." They also collaborate with other businesses and host Laksa evenings and monthly pizza nights. Amazing what three friends can do on the side!

Address 5 David's Road, SE 23 3EP, Tel +44(0)2082916646, stdavidcoffeehouse@gmail.com, www.stdavidcoffeehouse.co.uk | Getting there London Overground, Stop Forest Hill | Hours Tue–Thur 8am–5pm, Fri–Sat 8am–11pm, Sun 10am–4pm | Tip Combine shopping at the farmers' market with a visit to the Horniman Museum next door, which houses an aquarium, a collection of musical instruments, and a natural history exhibition. Great for kids!

93 Stepney City Farm Café
From barn to table

City farms have become important London institutions, supporting communities and motivating city dwellers to care for animals and plants. The city farm in Stepney has existed in various guises since the 1970s. With pigs, goats, and chickens; small garden plots that are rented by locals; and most of all a wonderful cafe, it attracts far more than just Stepney residents. In 2010, it became a registered charity and in 2013, the farm received some lottery funding and the cafe went from a small porter cabin to its current wood-clad bungalow-*cum*-loggia.

Relying almost entirely on volunteers, the cafe has only two full-time employees. Amy Goldstraw, having been a volunteer for years, became the manager when the new coffee shop launched in July 2013. It's open Tuesdays to Sundays and is busiest on the weekends. On Saturdays, Stepney locals do their shopping here at the farmers' market where there are stalls selling vegetables, fruit, bread, cheeses, meat, and cakes. They come for a coffee afterwards, which is made with beans provided by local roaster Climpson & Sons and organic milk from Goodwood's Farm in West Sussex.

Many customers return on Sundays to enjoy the now famous brunch, created by Joe, the other full-time staffer. He makes simple, good home-cooked dishes with the freshest ingredients. When they first opened, a lot of the food was still brought in, but now they cure their own bacon, make sausages and black pudding from scratch, churn butter, and bake sourdough bread. When they don't have enough meat, they source it ethically from the Ginger Pig, a local butcher. Fruit and vegetables are also either homegrown or come from Brockmans, an organic farm in Kent. The granola is homemade and most of the jams and pickles are as well. They also sell locally produced honey.

In 2014, Stepney City Farm Café was awarded "Best Eatery" by the Urban Food Awards.

Address Stepney Way, E 1 3DG, Tel +44(0)2077908204, info@stepneycityfarm.org, www.stepneycityfarm.org | Getting there Circle, District and Hammersmith & City Line, Stop Stepney Green | Hours Tue – Sun 10am – 4pm | Tip Have a look around the farm and watch the lovely Tamworth and Gloucester Old Spot pigs. They also have a resident blacksmith, potter, and woodworker here.

94_ Store Street Espresso

"Street–haunting" in Bloomsbury

Virginia Woolf used to walk all over London, watching people and imagining their lives. If she lived today, where would she go to write in her notebook? Well, since she lived in Bloomsbury, chances are she would have found herself on the pavement in front of Store Street Espresso. Store Street is one of the lesser-known shopping lanes in London, but it boasts many independent cafes and quirky stores. Surrounded by universities, it is mostly appreciated by students and academics.

In 2010, friends Rob and Jack founded Store Street Espresso, which has a modern, clean, and simple interior and a large concrete bar that was cast in situ. Rob had previously worked as a manager at Tinderbox cafe near Angel. Jack was a PhD student at University College London and understood the area well. They both saw great potential for a community coffee shop. "We could see that the coffee scene in London was changing and wanted to be a part of it," remembers Rob.

Recently they opened a second shop, called Continental Stores, on Tavistock Place, equipped with a kitchen so they can serve brunch and also bake cakes for the Store Street cafe. The house coffee here is provided by Square Mile, but on their second grinder they offer rotating guest coffees which come from London companies as well as roasters all over Europe. They use different brew methods for their coffee: bulk brew, pour-over, and, in the summer, cold brew as well.

The young scholars, professors, and local residents who come here for their daily coffee infusion can choose among muesli, granola, and toast for breakfast, and quiches, soups, and salads for brunch. A good selection of sweets, such as Guinness cake, cinnamon buns, and, in the winter, bread and butter pudding, is also on offer. Even if Virginia Woolf might not have ordered the former, she would definitely have enjoyed the atmosphere and the coffee.

STORE ST. ESPRESSO

Resident permit holders only
P
CA-E
Mon-Sat
8.30am-6.30pm

Address 40 Store Street, WC1E 7DB Tel +44(0)2076363011, info@storestespresso.co.uk, www.storestespresso.co.uk | **Getting there** Northern Line, Stop Goodge Street | **Hours** Mon–Fri 7.30am–7pm, Sat 9am–6pm, Sun 10am–5pm | **Tip** Senate House (Malet Street) is an imposing Art Deco building constructed between 1932 and 1937. In Senate House Library (4th to 18th floors), changing exhibitions are open to the public.

95__Story Coffee

All from one tree

This coffee shop is a welcome addition to the cafe scene in south-west London. Opened in September 2014, it is an incredibly light, stylish, and functional space, where you'll find superb coffee. Owners Sof and Jo didn't have any previous experience selling coffee when they opened Story, but they loved to drink it! Sof was working in marketing and decided to quit his career and do something he really enjoyed. "This is a local, community-focused cafe. We believe every coffee has a story to tell. That idea applies to other products as well. We want to give everything that we sell transparency."

Story uses the seasonal Red Brick espresso blend from Square Mile as its house blend, which is delivered twice a week. It also offers filter coffees and AeroPress. To make it more interesting for himself and his team, Sof sources beans from a variety of other roasters as well, such as Barn in Berlin and the Swedish company Drop. After all, that's why he opened a coffee shop in the first place: to experiment.

To achieve consistently high quality, the coffee is weighed twice during preparation. The milk from Goodwood Farm in Sussex gives the lattes and flat whites a super-smooth texture. You can also choose a Matcha latte – made from green tea powder and milk. Accompany it with a breakfast of brioche French toast with burnt banana, hazelnuts, and salted caramel, or Eggs Royale, with smoked salmon. Cakes come from a French bakery in Bermondsey.

Although the space is relatively modest in size, it is designed meticulously, down to the unique honeycomb pattern on the counter, and feels spacious thanks to the enormous windows and blond wood interior. Sof and Jo collaborated with a carpenter to make the furniture – and all the chairs and tables come from a single British elm tree. This is the type of unique detail that makes the cafe so enjoyable – after all, who doesn't like a great story?

Address 115 St John's Hill, SW11 1SZ, info@storycoffee.co.uk, www.storycoffee.co.uk | **Getting there** London Overground, Stop Clapham Junction | **Hours** Mon–Fri 7.30am–4.30pm, Sat–Sun 9am–5pm | **Tip** Le Gothique (The Royal Victoria Patriotic Building, John Archer Way) is a French restaurant in the heart of Wandsworth Common. It resides in an amazing historic building complete with courtyard.

96__ TAP Coffee No. 26

A winning formula

This cosy coffee shop is yet another gem in Fitzrovia's lively coffee community. There's no name on the plain grey façade, only "No. 26." Two benches and a painted black bicycle that's outfitted with a sign reading "coffee" sit in front of the cafe, and weather depending, you can find quite a crowd here, all enjoying their drinks in the sunshine.

The décor inside is simple, with wooden floors, tables, benches, and industrial lighting. Enticing fresh salads, pastries, sandwiches, and cakes are displayed near the entrance. The playing-card coffee labels attached with string to the retail packs of beans, quirky silver spoons, sugar served in old treacle tins, cute customer loyalty cards, and signs warning you not to feed the baristas, all indicate – even before you have your first sip of coffee – that this is a place where the staff pays lots of attention to detail. Opened in 2009 by Richard Lilley, No. 26 is now one of three TAP (formerly Tapped & Packed) coffee shops: No. 26 Rathbone Place, No. 114 Tottenham Court Road, and No. 193 Wardour Street.

Before starting the business, Richard visited several coffee houses in London and was convinced that he could do better. He designed every corner of this space himself, and from the start, he took an interest in the whole process of coffee production from farm to cup, so it naturally followed that TAP would roast its own coffee. The seasonal Jack of Spades blend has plum and red-currant notes mingled with milk chocolate and almond. They also roast single origins and serve them as espresso or filter, using V60, AeroPress, or siphon.

Winning the HYHOI's best coffee award in 2014 proves what meticulous attention they pay to their coffee. Add good food, including amazing brownies – with rotating flavours such as coconut macaroon or peanut butter – and sandwiches that are packed with interesting ingredients, and you have a winning formula.

Address 26 Rathbone Place, W1T 1JD, Tel (+44)02075802163, sales@tapcoffee.co.uk, www.tapcoffee.co.uk | **Getting there** Northern Line, Stop Tottenham Court Road | **Hours** Mon – Fri 8am – 7pm, Sat 10am – 6pm | **Tip** Did you know that St. Patrick's Church at Soho Square has extensive catacombs that spread under the square and beyond?

97_ Taylor St Baristas

Between steel and glass

In the world of cool steel and glass architecture at Harbour Exchange Square, Taylor St Baristas, South Quay, offers a warm wooden respite from the towering buildings and drafty spaces between them. Its customers are mostly office workers from the surrounding businesses, happy to have a quality cafe where they can spend their lunch break. Hungry coffee aficionados can order breakfast, fresh sandwiches, soups, quiches, pizzas, and delicious seasonal cakes, such as raspberry frangipane, all made daily in the kitchen.

The interior is spacious, with a huge front window on one side and a large counter made from different-coloured pieces of reclaimed wood on the other, all beautifully crafted by Wood Works in Brighton.

Taylor St. Baristas was founded in 2006 – a time before the coffee scene in London had taken hold – by Australian siblings Andrew, Laura, and Nick Tolley. Their business is named after Taylor Street, where they lived together in Sidney, because they wanted to enjoy the same quality of coffee and hospitality in the UK that they were used to back in Australia. The second part of the cafe's name indicates how much importance they place on the barista as a crucial link between customers and coffee. Taylor St Baristas now have nine coffee shops in London and Brighton and their staff receives extensive training.

Union Hand Roasted roasts the coffee for Taylor St, with a house espresso called Rogue Espresso, a seasonal blend they developed together. It has notes of jasmine, peach syrup, and citrus peel, but when combined with milk it develops flavours of sweet fudge, milk chocolate, and a hint of ginger. Their ever-changing guest espressos and filter coffees come from Square Mile, Has Bean, James Gourmet, and Union Hand Roasted. It's a challenge to preserve their individuality amidst so much competition, but the coffee served here remains a real treat for coffee lovers.

Address 1 Harbour Exchange Square, South Quay E 14 9GE, Tel +44(0)2030698833, southquay@taylor-st.com, www.taylor-st.com | Getting there DLR, Stop South Quay | Hours Mon–Fri 8am–5pm | Tip An early-morning trip to Billingsgate Market, the largest fish market in Europe (open 4am–9.30am, Trafalgar Way), will reward you with the freshest seafood possible.

98___Timberyard Seven Dials
Out of office

According to Darren Elliot, co-owner of Timberyard, communal workspaces are the new thing. This movement is further advanced in the United States where working nomadically is even more common. Darren's business partner, Ruth Turner, was working for Lloyds of London and knew from experience that there weren't many appealing spaces available in London to hold business meetings. So together they founded Timberyard in Old Street in 2012. And in 2014 they added the cafe in Seven Dials with rooms downstairs and upstairs.

Work is actively encouraged here: there are sockets and charging stations everywhere and iPads are available to customers. The music level is low, just loud enough to mask conversation. Customers use the downstairs area when they require deeper concentration, while the upstairs is more "vibey."

The workspace here is good, but the cafe also has a lot to offer: the house espresso blend is Jabberwocky by Has Bean and there's specialty tea from Waterloo Tea in Cardiff, with blends such as Iron Goddess Oolong and Tangerine Ginger. "Tea has been very overlooked in the last few years, considering we are supposed to be a nation of tea drinkers. We've devoted half of the menu to tea. People drink coffee in the morning and switch to tea in the afternoon." There is an all-day breakfast menu; salads and sandwiches are made fresh on-site and are mostly vegetarian. Pop-tarts, peanut-butter brownies, and other delicious cakes are provided by Bittersweet Bakers. Bread comes from Seven Seeded Bakery and the pastry from Yeast.

Recently, Timberyard won several awards, among them one for London's Best Café for Out-of-Office Workers, and another for Best Independent Coffee Shop in Europe. No wonder there are plans to open more venues in London. The next location will open in Soho, with a private members' floor and brew bar.

Cherry & Almond Tart

Apricot Tart

Chocolate Cookie

Orange + Honey & Polenta Loaf

3·20

G.F.

Zucc. Coo.

3·20

Bana Loa

Address 7 Upper St Martin's Lane, WC2H 9DL, hello@timberyardlondon.com,
www.timberyardlondon.com | Getting there Piccadilly Line, Stop Covent Garden |
Hours Mon–Fri 8am–8pm, Sat–Sun 10am–8pm | Tip Coffee aficionados can also
visit Monmouth Coffee (Monmouth Street), one of the pioneers of the resurgent
coffee movement in the UK.

99__Tina, We Salute You

Coffee and culture in Dalston

On a rainy, miserable, cold winter day in Dalston, a visit to Tina's can have life-saving qualities. The cafe invariably cheers you up with its ever-changing art exhibitions and Tina herself, the iconic sultry lady who has been the shop's mascot since its early days as a cupcake stall near Brick lane. Co-owner Steve Hawks explains that they had her hanging on the booth because she was "all retro and naf as cupcakes are." They eventually learned she was a real woman called Tina, painted by mass-market artist J. H. Lynch in the 1960s. When the coffee shop opened in 2009, she came with it.

Before Steve founded the cafe together with Danny Bolton, he lived several years in Melbourne and was influenced by the local coffee scene there. Today, through the loving oversight of its owners, Tina's has become a hub for artistic talent and coffeehouse culture in the area. Every three months, the walls in the shop are painted over and a new artist is given free reign to transform the space. An outside wall also is used as a canvas. Often staff members don't even know what the next artist will create, and arrive one morning to find a completely "new" cafe.

Tina has many loyal regulars who live in the neighborhood, but the shop also attracts customers from all over London. Apart from the art, the lovingly prepared food is a big draw. Cakes are baked fresh every day: try a piece of the delicious Victoria sponge or the more unusual fig-and-raspberry-jam slice, or a chocolatine. Their brunchlike menu ranges from American-style pancakes to the "Porker": pulled pork and Polish sausage on sourdough toast.

Most of all, people come here for the coffee itself. Tina's espresso house blend from Alchemy has chocolate, hazelnut, and red currant notes. They also sell beans from the Roasting Shed, made by their own resident roaster. All in all, it's a winning combination: coffee and culture in Dalston!

Address 47 King Henry's Walk, N1 4NH, Tel +44(0)2031190047, tinawesaluteyou.com |
Getting there London Overground to Richmond or Stratford, Stop Dalston Kingsland |
Hours Mon–Fri 8am–6pm, Sat–Sun 10am–6pm | **Tip** Check out Ridley Road Market
(just opposite Dalston Kingsland Station), where you can get everything from exotic fruit
to African fabrics.

100__ Tomtom Coffee House

Havana in Belgravia

Picture this: it's a mild summer evening, you are sitting in front of a lovely cafe, and you are drinking an excellent coffee with one hand while puffing a Cuban Havana with the other. That's the vision owner Tom Assheton had in mind when he launched Tomtom Coffee House. Inspired by a journey to Cuba, Tom wanted to combine cigars and coffee. When he found a space on Elisabeth Street, however, it wasn't big enough for both, so he set up the cigar store first.

Years later he finally realised his dream and opened a cafe opposite the smoke shop. For the best coffee possible, Tom teamed up with roaster Giles Dick-Read, who has a roasting facility in Dorset. The cafe's head barista explains that Giles roasts new batches of their unique espresso blend every week. They use 100 percent Arabica beans that are sourced from four different countries: Nicaragua, Indonesia, Guatemala, and Brazil. They roast in small batches with frequency to ensure freshness and quality. You can buy the blend and single origins from 14 different countries in the shop or on their website. They will also grind the beans to your specification and method of preparation. A selection of teas is available as well, "perfectly brewed and served as tea should be."

Coffee and cigars are the major players here, but for those who can't live on these two indulgences alone, there's a breakfast menu with several different egg dishes, pancakes, fruit, and yoghurt; butties, salads, toasties, and tartines are offered at lunch; and home-baked cakes, flapjacks, and brownies are available all day. Cakes and salads are all made downstairs in the kitchen, and in the evening, they offer a cheese board and a cured-meat selection. To accompany your plate, you can choose among different wines from the legendary Berry Brothers in St James, or have a Bavarian-style draft beer. And of course, you are more than welcome to enjoy a cigar at one of the outdoor cafe tables.

Address 114 Ebury Street, SW1W 9QD, Tel +44(0)2077301771, coffee@tomtom.co.uk, www.tomtom.co.uk | **Getting there** Circle, District and Victoria Line, Stop Victoria or Sloane Square | **Hours** Mon–Fri 8am–6pm, Sat–Sun 9am–6pm | **Tip** Two doors down the road (116 Ebury Street), Peggy Porschen sells delightful cakes and biscuits in an all-pink shop.

101 Tried & True

Kiwi brunches in Putney

This cafe on Upper Richmond Road in Putney is a little bit off the beaten track, but if you're on your way to Richmond Park or the London Wetland Centre, it's the perfect place to stop for breakfast or brunch.

New Zealander Rob Kelley founded Tried & True in 2010. When he opened in this former gallery space, there was no real kitchen and the cafe served only sandwiches. Now they've developed a substantial all-day breakfast/brunch menu and have won several accolades for their food. One of the award-winning dishes is the Pulled Pork Benedict: pork in hickory hoisin sauce served on homemade jalapeno cheddar cornbread with two poached eggs, chilli butter, and spring onions. Obviously cyclists would find this meal fortifying before or after a ride and therefore the dish is a big seller over the weekend. Also very popular are the buttermilk pancakes with seasonal compote, mascarpone, and maple syrup, made to order.

There are many egg dishes on the menu and the team here goes through 1,000 organic eggs a week, which are provided by Rookery Farm. A healthier option is the toasted muesli with Greek yoghurt and seasonal compote. The bread and pastry come from Seven Seeded Bakers, cakes from Galeta, and meat from a butcher in the area where Rob lives. There is a lot of emphasis on good food here, but that doesn't mean the coffee is neglected. They use the Red Brick seasonal blend from Square Mile.

By now an increasing number of locals have discovered the quality coffee and epic breakfasts. "Regulars started to come in once a week; that turned into two to three times a week, and then once or more a day." For Tried & True's manager, this is not only due to the success of the menu but also to good service. "We like to think that's an element we do particularly well." Even Nick Clegg, who lives nearby, pops in to enjoy the Kiwi brunches.

TRIED & TRUE

Address 279 Upper Richmond Road, SW15 6SP, Tel +44(0)2087890410, info@triedandtruecafe.co.uk, www.triedandtruecafe.co.uk | **Getting there** District Line, Stop East Putney | **Hours** Mon – Fri 8am – 4pm, Sat – Sun 8.30am – 4.30pm | **Tip** Visit nearby London Wetland Centre (Queen Elizabeth's Walk) for some bird watching.

102 TwoDoorsDown
A cafe with a kick

A few nice, independent cafes have sprouted up recently in this area, but none better than TwoDoorsDown. A lot of Kentish Towners obviously think so as well, since they immediately became regulars here when the cafe opened in May 2014.

This coffee shop is a dream come true for Klara and Rich Bernatt–Williams, but one they hadn't expected to realise for at least another 10 years. Rich trained as a barista 12 years ago, which led to an ongoing obsession with coffee, although in subsequent years he worked as a designer and photographer in the same school where Klara was employed as an English teacher. When Klara's mum unfortunately passed away, however, they came into a small inheritance, gave up their jobs and went after their dream.

So far, it's working out splendidly. For espresso-based drinks, they use the Redchurch Blend by Allpress to guarantee consistency and give customers the opportunity to always have their favourite coffee. They also do single-origin guest filters – which they change every fortnight – from 10 to 12 different specialty roasters all over London and beyond, with coffees from Bristol or Newcastle. They use V60 or AeroPress to make the coffee to order.

For breakfast, Klara's homemade granola and various choices of topped toast are on the menu, and Rich makes a signature dish that seduces locals into becoming regulars. He started with a quail-egg sausage roll "with a kick," a cross between a scotch egg and a sausage roll. They proved so popular that he invented others: Black Pudding and Apple Sauce, Chunky Piccalilli, Pig Wellington, and All Day Breakfast – black pudding and scrambled eggs wrapped in bacon and served with Bloody Mary ketchup.

It's obvious that Klara and Rich are having great fun. When asked if things turned out the way they expected, their answer comes quickly: "No, it's better!"

Address 73 Kentish Town Road, NW1 8NY, Tel +44(0)7889058585, twodoorsdown@outlook.com, www.twodoorsdowncoffee.co.uk | **Getting there** Northern Line, Stop Camden Town | **Hours** Mon–Fri 7.30am–7pm, Sat 8.30am–6pm, Sun 9.30am–5.30pm | **Tip** For a traditional English pie & mash, go to Castles Pie Shop (229 Royal College Street).

103_Vagabond N7

From farm to cup

Dainoras Petrauskas has come a long way. The owner and co–founder of Vagabond began life in Lithuania and was educated there as a ballet dancer. He worked in construction for several years in London, where he acquired carpentry skills. Eventually he took a job as a barista for Tapped & Packed, learned the coffee business, and opened his first shop in Stroud Green Vagabond N4 together with his nephew in 2011. The Holloway Road shop followed in 2013, and their latest venture, Vagabond E 1, is within the Cass (John Cass Faculty of Art and Architecture) in Whitechapel.

Vagabond offers Dainoras the perfect platform for his creativity. He designed and built all the fittings in the cafe himself. The tables in the back room are made of former scaffolding boards that hang on chains from the ceiling. He also screens films here, hosts painting classes, exhibitions, and live music, and does cupping sessions. The food is tasty and simple: eggs, omelettes, soups, and sandwiches. The cakes are homemade from recipes developed by Dainoras when a bicycle accident forced him to be housebound for a few weeks.

But coffee is the one thing he's really passionate about and he expects the same attitude from his baristas, who undergo extensive training. "A lot of people see it only as a job, but we want more from our baristas. There is room here to grow." There's a trend in coffee now to trace beans back to their roots, making every step of their journey from farm to cup transparent. One of Dainoras's baristas, Anthony, took up the challenge and cycled to Ethiopia.

Vagabond has begun roasting its own blends. One espresso blend they've created contains 30 percent El Salvador, 30 percent Brazil, and 30 percent Ethiopian beans. To taste it, order an Espresso Flight, which includes a flat white and an espresso, each with a single shot of coffee. They also offer single-origin brew coffee and cold brew coffee.

Address 105 Holloway Road, N7 8LT, info@vagabond.london, www.vagabond.london | **Getting there** London Overground, Stop Highbury & Islington | **Hours** Mon–Sat 7am–6pm, Sat–Sun 9am–6pm | **Tip** Just a few steps away, St Mary Magdalene Church has a lovely garden, which you can enjoy with your takeaway coffee on a beautiful day.

104__Village Café
All in the family

On York Rise in residential Dartmouth Park, you'll find a few shops servicing the local community. This is the home of Village Café, opened by owner Nico Ozdemir in 2011. Right next to the cafe is a grocery shop, which also belongs to Nico's family and which he runs with his uncle. Family plays a central role in Nico's life. He comes from a small village in Turkey and grew up on a farm, so to him, fresh food is essential. "I just love it and believe that you have to create something from out of yourself to become successful."

Nico constantly invents new dishes for his own pleasure – but also enjoys sharing them with his customers. When you place an order here, it is very likely that you will also be served a taste of his newly created "spice potato salad" or some other dish he is working on. Whatever it is, try it: it will be delicious! The food is largely Mediterranean and Nico's specialities are barbeques such as Kofte, Lamb Sis, and Kebab – all with very generous portions of salad. The menu also offers a range of all-day breakfast options, from eggs Benedict to a Mediterranean breakfast. There's also porridge and a lovely yoghurt with honey and fruit. Pastries are baked here every morning and there are always one or two cakes – such as chocolate cake, carrot cake, or pear tart – that Nico bakes himself. All ingredients come from his shop next door.

The London Roaster Moka provides the coffee beans at Village Café. Other beverages include lemon and lime or orange and pomegranate juices, pressed right before your eyes. Nico named his business because of the "village" feel of the area: "I know everyone and everyone knows me." Take a seat on the pavement in front of the cafe, enjoy the small-town vibe, and let Nico create something for you. You might even spot Labour politician Ed Milliband and his wife, who regularly visit the local shop and have even given interviews here.

Address 20 York Rise, NW5 1SR, Tel +44(0)2074823392, www.facebook.com/pages/Village-Cafe-York-Rise/632629086795507 | **Getting there** Northern Line, Stop Tufnell Park | **Hours** Mon–Sun 8am–6pm | **Tip** Opposite the Village Café, Truffles Delicatessen sells delicious ham and freshly made pasta.

105 Volcano Coffee Works

Coffee obsessed

Kurt Stewart, master roaster and co-founder of Volcano Coffee Works, is an inexhaustible source of knowledge when it comes to coffee. Did you know, for example, that it takes about 300 pairs of hands to make a single cup of espresso?

All the coffee in the world is grown between the tropics of Cancer and Capricorn in an area called the Bean Belt. Kurt uses high-mountain Arabica beans that are slow growing with low yields, but with an intense flavour. He sources from five green bean suppliers but also has direct contact with coffee growers in El Salvador and Nicaragua. The roastery produces their signature espresso blend, Fullsteam, with notes of almond, spice tobacco and liquorice, and Mount, which pays homage to Kurt's father, with low acidity, a cocoa body, and notes of light spice. They also make a seasonal blend, changing at each equinox and solstice, and about 23 single origins that can be used with different extraction methods. Kurt has a foible for machines, especially Italian ones, and the roastery next to the shop is filled with beautiful old Italian roasters. They currently use a Vittoria 30kg roaster that was built in the 1950s.

Kurt is from New Zealand and was trained as a professional chef but couldn't continue to work as one after a motorbike accident. He'd always dabbled in coffee and this seemed the way to go. He started his new professional journey in style: with a three-wheeled 1940s Piaggio Ape coffee cart. In 2010, he established Volcano Coffee Works together with his friend Olaf. More and more visitors to the roastery wanted espressos or flat whites so when Kurt and his team were offered cafe space in the same building – which houses around 100 small business – they took the opportunity to showcase their coffees.

Most customers come from the surrounding businesses or are coffee aficionados eager to try the delicious roasts made by the truly coffee-obsessed.

Address Unit F 01, Ground Floor, Parkhall Trading Estate, 40 Martell Road, SE 21 8EN, Tel +44(0)2086708927 | **Getting there** Victoria Line to Brixton, Bus 322 towards Crystal Palace Parade, Stop Martell Road | **Hours** Mon–Fri 8am–4pm, Sat 9am–4pm | **Tip** Walk to Norwood Park for some amazing views across London.

106_ Wild & Wood Coffee

Packed with originality

It's only 249 square feet, but this little coffee shop is packed with originality. Wood panelling and church pews form the backdrop for a collection of photographs depicting old-time British comedians. Its unique decor transports you back in time. Co-owner Adalat Hussain, who admits to being a grumpy guy, put the photographs up because he likes looking at them: "When you switch on the television, the world is full of violence, but when I see all the lovely characters of yesteryear, it makes me feel happy to be here." His love for old crockery – which he buys at auctions and displays (and sells) in the shop – contributes to the special atmosphere of the place.

Founded in 2008, Wild & Wood has served Monmouth coffee from the start. Adalat objects to people who say they have a passion for this or that. "That's just nonsense. I have a passion for my wife and I make very good coffee!" As well as the special blend they get from Monmouth, they use Brazilian beans. Their aim is to keep the quality consistent and to work with the best ingredients. For the coffee, this means serving it with Jersey organic milk. The cakes and pastries are from Sally Clarke and Cocomaya, two of the finest bakers in town. Try the different kinds of "cronuts," a cross between a croissant and a doughnut, in flavours such as tiramisu, cheesecake, or cinnamon.

In 2013, Wild & Wood won the London Lifestyle Award for best coffee shop. And according to Adalat, it's also the cheapest artisan cafe around. During the week customers mainly come from the surrounding offices, but on the weekends couples and families drop by, and most of them are regulars. Adalat believes that it pays to keep the quality of his products high, as his customers are very savvy and have equally high expectations. Visitors also appreciate Adalat's tendency to speak his mind. After all, he is over 50 years old now and has earned the right to say whatever he wants—in a nice way of course!

Address 47 London Wall, EC2M 5TE, Tel +44(0)7525155957, www.wildandwoodcoffee.co.uk | Getting there Circle, Hammersmith & City, Metropolitan and Northern Line, Stop Moorgate | Hours Mon–Fri 7.30am–5.45pm, Sat 10am–5.30pm, Sun 10am–3pm | Tip Visit the nearby City of London Police Museum (37 Wood Street), which offers many interesting exhibits, among them a miniature Tardis and bombs that were created by the Suffragettes.

107_The Wilton Way Café
Tune in and chill out

This beautifully designed space on a quiet street in Hackney houses not only a great coffee shop but also a radio station called London Fields. The interior, with its round light blue counters made from corrugated iron sheets and multi-coloured lamps, was conceived by a local design duo called the Dog and Wardrobe. The radio station occupies its own little counter at the front of the cafe and is visible from the street. Programs are recorded while customers drink coffee and chat in the background.

The Wilton Way Café and London Fields Radio are co-owned by Dominik Prosser and David McHugh. They were established in 2010 as a focal point for the community: meant to give a voice and a platform to local artists, musicians, and designers. The radio station, which is manned by two people, broadcasts podcasts twice a day which are also available on their website. The programs touch a wide range of subjects, themes, and interests, all of which reflect the neighbourhood's sensibilities. The station's live broadcasts of the street parties at Wilton Way have become famous in Hackney and beyond. The cafe also hosts exhibitions of area artists.

Of course, coffee plays an all-important role too. They use Climpson & Sons coffee beans, which can be purchased in the shop as well. The menu is simple and all the ingredients are sourced as locally as possible. The cheese is from Neal's Yard and chorizo from Brindisa in Borough; pastry comes from Seven Seeded Bakery, and cakes are provided by Melza Bean Bakery and Violet's Cakes. Very popular among the locals is the Lido breakfast, made with organic oats, Greek yoghurt, fresh fruit, and honey. At lunchtime, go for a more "brunchy" option, such as portobello mushrooms on garlic toast with rocket and goat's cheese or avocado on sourdough with lemon and chilli. And enjoy it all while listening to your favourite radio show.

Address 63 Wilton Way, E 8 1BG, www.londonfieldsradio.co.uk | **Getting there** London Overground, Stop Hackney Central | **Hours** Mon–Fri 8am–5pm, Sat 8am–6pm, Sun 9am–6pm | **Tip** Enjoy a swim in the London Fields Lido (London Fields West Side).

108__Workshop Coffee Co.

A career in coffee

The Fitzrovia Coffeebar of Workshop Coffee Co. is a small but beautifully designed space with lots of attention to detail. There is a counter topped with iridescent Madagascan granite, parquet floor, a standing area in the front of the cafe, and secluded seating in the back. The light blue rippled pressed-glass lampshades throw interesting patterns on the blue and green walls. Naturally, the coffee machine is a Marzocco Linea PB and carries the name of the cafe in golden letters. The coffee menu is simple: they serve Cult of Done espresso, cappuccino, latte, and two different filter coffees made with AeroPress and Fetco CBS brewers. The coffee is served graciously on a small wooden tray with a glass of water. They also have a limited selection of delicious sandwiches – such as pesto and mozzarella, pastries, and cakes, sourced from Yeast, Little Bread Pedlar, and Sally White.

Who put so much attention into all this detail? Workshop's founder James Dickson, who has a professional background as a chartered surveyor. He had an interest in coffee and followed the evolution of the third wave coffee movement around the world long before he opened the first cafe and roastery in a Victorian textile factory in Clerkenwell, in 2011. His vision was to combine Australian coffee culture with European sourcing and roasting methods, creating "a vertically integrated coffee company."

Before he opened the business, James spent time with coffee farmers in Africa and Central America, building relationships with partners in producing countries. There are four Workshop Coffee shops in London now and they sell coffee beans on their website and in the cafes. The roasting is all done at the Clerkenwell cafe, which sells more than 4,000 cups of hot beverages per week. "If you wanted to make a career in coffee six to eight years ago, you could not really do it. Now it's possible."

Address 80 Mortimer St, W1W 7FE, fitzrovia@workshopcoffee.com, www.workshopcoffee.com | **Getting there** Bakerloo, Central and Victoria Line, Stop Oxford Circus | **Hours** Mon–Fri 7am–7pm, Sat–Sun 9am–6pm | **Tip** Do you love Georgian architecture? Book a room at Chandos House (2 Queen Anne Street). Neo-classicism can't get much better than this hotel, built in the 18th century by Robert Adam.

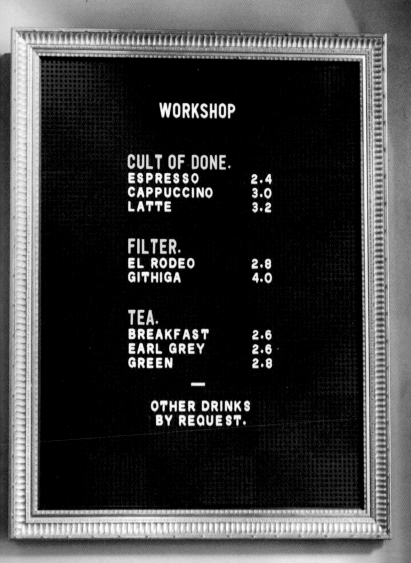

109_ The Wren

A new reason to go to church

Undoubtedly, the Wren boasts the highest ceiling of any coffee shop in London. It's an amazing experience to sit in this cavernous room and watch the light filter through the stained-glass windows as you enjoy a cappuccino and a gingerbread man. The enormous counter is clad in a wooden version of Christopher Wren's plan for medieval London after the Great Fire of 1666. Wren's plan was never realized because it called for the demolition of even more buildings, which was considered too expensive and time-consuming by Wren's contemporaries. However, Wren did undertake the design of 51 city churches. From 1671 to 1681, his firm rebuilt St Nicholas Cole Abbey, which dates back to the 12th century and which the cafe now occupies.

The church had been unused for over a decade when it was renovated by the Church of England. It is used now by "St Nick's Talks," a Christian ministry group that has offices here. They gave Sam Priestley and Andrew Holt permission to build a cafe on the premises. The two had toyed for quite a while with the idea of opening a coffee shop in a church – and were finally able to realize their vision.

Sam and Andrew engaged Olivia Adshead, who had plenty of coffee bar experience, to set up and run the cafe. The Wren finally opened in March 2014 and did so well in the first few weeks that it won the award for "London's best new coffee shop." The beans come from Workshop and are delivered every week by bike. They have their own chef who bakes most of the cakes and makes the sandwiches, soups, quiches, and stews featured on the menu.

On Thursdays, the ministry group holds a weekly Bible talk; other events include conferences and lectures. The church can also be rented for weddings since it is still consecrated and even has a vicar. In 1968 it was used as a location for the *Doctor Who* episode "The Invasion." It doesn't get cooler than that!

Address 114 Queen Victoria Street, EC4V 4BJ, Tel +44(0)2072361014,
info@thewrencoffee.com, www.thewrencoffee.com | Getting there Circle and District Line,
Stop Mansion House | Hours Mon–Fri 7am–5pm | Tip Walk to St Paul's Cathedral,
which also fell victim to the Great Fire. It took Wren 45 years to rebuild it!

110_Zealand Road Coffee
Roman Road revival

One hundred years ago, Roman Road was called Drift Street, but then an archaeological dig uncovered remains of the old Roman road to Colcester, and it was renamed. Roman Road is known for its street market filled with cheap but trendy clothes, household items, make-up, jewellery, and a food court on St Stephen's Road. A bit further away from the hustle and bustle of the market at the corner of Zealand Road, a small corner cafe has established a reputation for good coffee, friendly service, and pleasant food.

When owners Rachael Young and Laurie Hoskin opened the coffee shop in 2011, this was still a neglected stretch of road with many empty shops. The partners wanted to create a neighbourhood cafe with the kind of relaxed, warm atmosphere they'd experienced when living in Melbourne. It was a risk and they had only a tiny budget, but local residents immediately embraced the cafe. "The most enjoyable aspect of running ZRC for me is the customers. I think that's the advantage of being a neighbourhood place; it comes with a sense of familiarity which makes people feel at home."

Zealand Road's coffee comes from the Cornwall roaster Origin. The food menu changes every few weeks and offers different breakfast options, such as Bircher Muesli with fresh berries, and Bacon Buttie as well as other sandwiches and flatbreads. The cakes are sourced from a local bakery. And to keep it more interesting for their customers, Zealand Road also exhibits guest art collections, which change every few months.

At the end of 2014, the cafe closed briefly for refurbishment but was back in 2015 with renewed energy. In the last few years, more and more shops and cafes have cropped up around them. On nice-weather days, the locals sit at tables on the pavement outside the cafe, read newspapers, enjoy their coffee, and watch Roman Road coming back to life.

Address 391 Roman Road, E 3 5QS, Tel +44(0)2088806988,
www.facebook.com/zealandroadcoffeeshop | **Getting there** Central, Circle, District
and Hammersmith & City Line, Stop Mile End. From here, walk or take bus 339
toward Leytonstone Grove Green, Stop Roman Road Grove Road. | **Hours** Mon–Fri
8am–5pm, Sat–Sun 9am–5pm | **Tip** Do your shopping at Roman Road Market
(Tue, Thur 10am–4pm, Sat 9am–5pm).

111__Ziferblat

Whatever you want it to be

In Russian and German, *ziferblatt* means the face of a clock. "Ziferblat is not a cafe," clarifies the manager of the venue's events program. "It is a pay-by-minute co-working space." When you arrive, you ring a buzzer and go up to the first floor. You clock in and at the end of your stay you pay for the time spent here. Everything else is free.

There's a large comfortable room with eclectic furniture and spotted wallpaper. Art installations decorate the walls and ceiling and a blackboard announces the week's events. You can sit at any table you like and use the free Wi-Fi or browse the books. If you get hungry or thirsty, just go to the small kitchen, make yourself a coffee or tea, take a biscuit, cake, or piece of fruit, eat a bowl of cornflakes, or make some toast. You can also bring your own food and store it in the fridge as long as you clean up after yourself.

Ziferblat is the brainchild of Ivan Mitin, a Russian poet. He and his friends were looking for someplace where they could talk, work, and socialize together. They found a small space in Moscow and called it Treehouse. It survived on contributions and became so popular that they eventually had to expand and rent a bigger space that couldn't subsist on donations alone. So Mitin came up with the pay-per-minute system. Ziferblat now has 14 locations all over the world; the latest one is in Manchester.

Who patronizes Ziferblat? "In Shoreditch, we get mainly artists that have no space at home or feel isolated," says the manager. "We are networking facilitators and bring people together. We talk to them, find out what they need, and match them up." They also run yoga and art classes, music sessions, throw parties, host talks, and organise speed-dating events. "Whatever it needs to be for you it can be!" Ziferblat may not be a cafe in the conventional sense, but it does what the best of them do.

Address 388 Old Street, EC1V 9LT, Tel +44(0)7984693440, ziferblat.london@gmail.com, www.ziferblat.net | Getting there Northern Line, Stop Old Street | Hours Mon–Fri 10am–11pm, Sat–Sun 12pm–11pm | Tip In Leila's Shop (15–17 Calvert Avenue) you can get fresh fruit and vegetables, but also very good coffee.

Glossary of Coffee Terms

AeroPress device for brewing coffee in which the coffee is steeped briefly and then pressed through a filter

Americano an espresso with hot water added

Arabica / robusta coffee beans two different commercially used coffee beans. Arabica beans are more flavourful, while robusta beans contain double the amount of caffeine. Arabica grows best at higher altitudes; the plants are more delicate than robusta and have a higher susceptibility to disease.

Blend a mixture of two or more single-origin coffees

Cold-brew coffee brewing method whereby ground coffee is steeped in lukewarm or cold water for a long period of time (usually 12 hours or more)

Cortado an espresso with a small amount of warm milk

Crema light brown foam covering the surface of a good, fresh espresso

Doppio a double-shot espresso

Espresso flight a single-shot espresso and a single-shot cappuccino served side by side

Extraction percentage of coffee grounds that are dissolved in water

Flat white espresso with steamed milk (micro foam)

Latte art patterns that are formed by pouring steamed milk into espresso-based drinks

Micro foam milk foam containing tiny bubbles used for making latte art

Mocha espresso with steamed milk and chocolate or chocolate syrup

Pour-over brewing method whereby hot water is poured over a filter with ground coffee in a filter holder. There are various pour-over coffeemakers on the market, among them the Chemex and the Hario V60.

Ristretto a very short espresso shot with half the water of a normal shot

Strictly hard bean/strictly soft bean method of grading coffee beans based on the elevation they come from. Higher elevation beans are harder (more dense) and considered better quality.

Single-origin coffee beans that are grown in a single geographic location, be it a farm, region, or country

Sweet spot roasting point at which the acidity and caramelization of the coffee beans are perfectly balanced

Third wave coffee refers to artisan coffees produced by independent coffee establishments

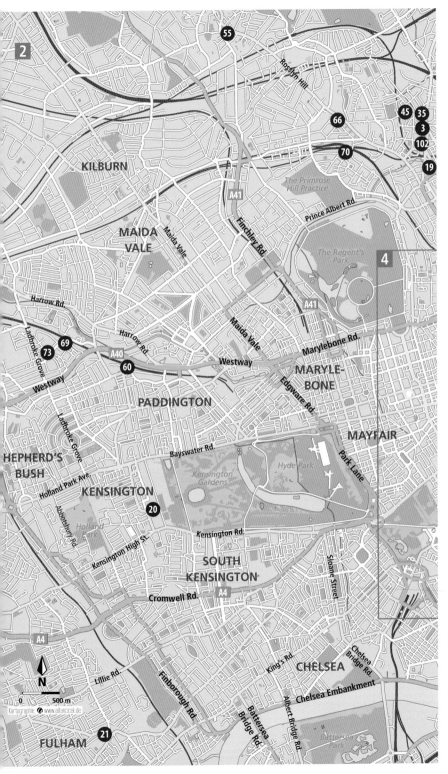

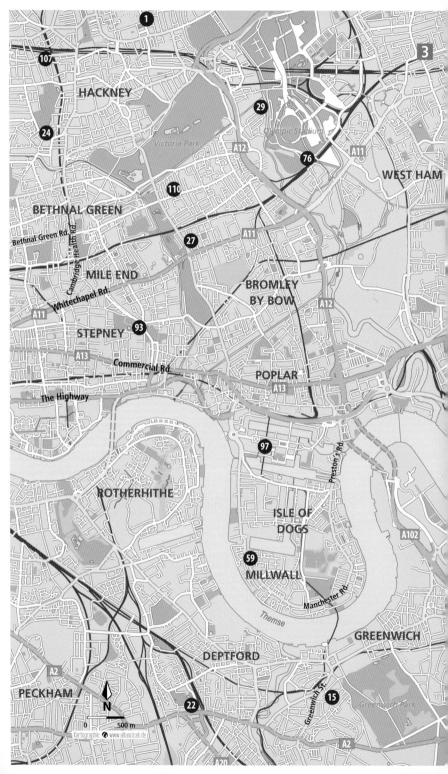

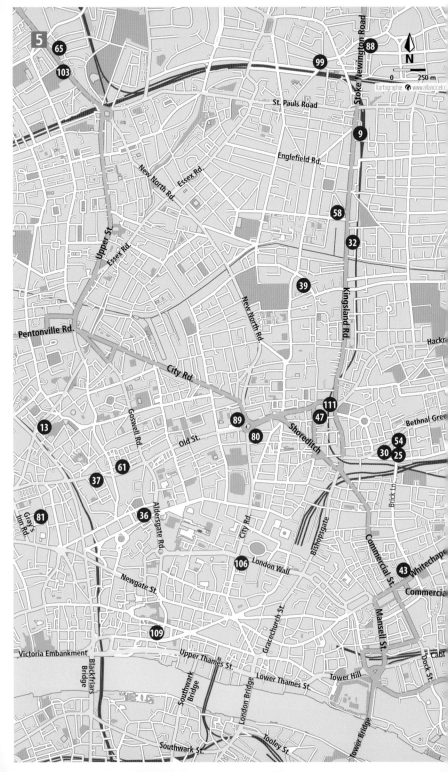

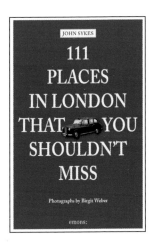

John Sykes, Birgit Weber
**111 Places in London
That You Shouldn't Miss**
ISBN 978-3-95451-346-8

Kirstin von Glasow
**111 Shops in London
That You Shouldn't Miss**
ISBN 978-3-95451-341-3

Kirstin von Glasow was born and raised in Cologne, and studied German literature, philosophy, and art history. Today she works as a curator, writer, and filmmaker in London. She is the author of *111 Shops in London That You Shouldn't Miss* (Emons).

Find an online map of the coffee shops here: